Phallos

Marie-Louise von Franz, Honorary Patron

**Studies in Jungian Psychology
by Jungian Analysts**

Daryl Sharp, General Editor

PHALLOS

Sacred Image of the Masculine

Eugene Monick

I thank Barbara Monick, the Union Graduate School, Alice Petersen, Doris Albrecht, Bonnie Strohl, ARAS, Library of the C.G. Jung Institute-Zurich, Alexander McCurdy, James Hillman, John Walsh, Lala Zeitlyn, Dorcas Bankes, Jonathan Goldberg, my analysands and many others.
I thank my father.

Canadian Cataloguing in Publication Data

Monick, Eugene A. (Eugene Arthur), 1929-
  Phallos : sacred image of the masculine

(Studies in Jungian psychology by Jungian analysts; 27)

Bibliography: p.

Includes index.

ISBN 0-919123-26-0

1. Penis—Psychological aspects.   2. Phallicism.
3. Maculinity (Psychology).   I. Title.   II. Series.

BF692.5.M65 1987   155.3'32   C86-095084-0

INNER CITY BOOKS
Box 1271, Station Q, Toronto, Canada M4T 2P4
Telephone (416) 927-0355

Honorary Patron: Marie-Louise von Franz.
Publisher and General Editor: Daryl Sharp.
Editorial Board: Fraser Boa, Daryl Sharp, Marion Woodman.
Executive Assistants: Vicki Cowan, Ben Sharp.

INNER CITY BOOKS was founded in 1980 to promote the understanding and practical application of the work of C.G. Jung.

Front Cover: God's Cock (the masculine wakening the feminine part of the psyche), by Margaret Jacoby-Lopez (1978). Reproduced courtesy the artist. (Collection Mr. and Mrs. Richard Gill, Perth, Australia)

Back Cover: Satyr, 5th century B.C. (From the Karapanos Collection, National Archaeological Museum, Athens)

Index by Daryl Sharp

Printed and bound in Canada by
University of Toronto Press Incorporated

CONTENTS

See final pages for descriptions of other Inner City Books

Illustration Credits

New points of view are not as a rule discovered in
territory that is already known, but in out-of-the-way
places that may even be avoided because of their bad name.
—C.G. Jung, *Synchronicity: An Acausal Connecting Principle.*

In the struggle against paganism . . . sanctity became sodomy,
worship became fornication, and so on. . . . Judaism and Christianity
between them—and this includes Freud—have had a heavy
and disastrous hand in this misunderstanding. . . . An age whose eyes
are once more open to the transpersonal must reverse this process.
—Erich Neumann, *The Origins and History of Consciousness.*

Ithyphallic figure, with phallos as waterspout.
(House of the Vettii, Pompeii, 1st cent. A.D.)

Introduction

Men need to understand the psychological underpinnings of their gender and their sexuality better than they do. One might think that in a patriarchal society males would grasp the basis of masculine identity naturally and spontaneously. They usually do not.

For many men, the dominance of the masculine is taken for granted, so familiar is their experience of superior status. But for an increasing number, masculinity is as much an enigma as femininity. These men do not easily make assumptions about themselves and their behavior and place in life. They feel that something is missing in their psychological situation, and they come to therapy to correct it. What they are given, often, are definitions of masculinity that only obliquely address the disjuncture they feel in their lives. These men are masculine, but they are beyond the reach of the patriarchy. Even men who know themselves to be safely within the patriarchal framework know that something is amiss, that the old order is passing away.

There is a lack of contemporary Jungian writing about masculine issues in general, and almost nothing, since Erich Neumann's *Origins and History of Consciousness,* on the archetypal basis of masculinity. My suspicion is that the lacuna is a result of the dominance of patriarchal attitudes in psychoanalysis, including Jung's analytical psychology. One does not write about that which seems to be obvious. The problem is that patriarchal attitudes and values are no longer obviously true. Unless masculinity is differentiated from patriarchy, both will go down the drain together.

To write of archetypal masculinity means to concentrate upon phallos, the erect penis, the emblem and standard of maleness. All images through which masculinity is defined have phallos as their point of reference. Sinew, determination, effectuality, penetration, straightforwardness, hardness, strength—all have phallos giving them effect. Phallos is the fundamental mark of maleness, its stamp, its impression. Erection points to a powerful inner reality at work in a man, not altogether in his control. This inner reality may be different from a man's conscious desires at a given time. Phallos is subjective authority for a male, and objective for those who come into contact with him. This is what makes phallos archetypal. No male has to learn phallos. It presents itself to him, as a god does.

9

A male uses phallos; he is not a man if he cannot do so. Men need to know their source of authority and to respect their sacred symbol. Phallos opens the door to masculine depth.

Phallos has been neglected as an originating psychic force within the literature of psychoanalysis. It has been suggested by the fathers but not developed as a primal element in the psyche. Psychoanalytic theory, whether Freudian or Jungian, gives singular primacy to the mother as the basis of life. This is an error.

The lack of phallic participation in theories of origin forces phallos into distorting compensations to make itself felt and realized within therapy. Phallos does not submit easily. Patriarchal attitudes dominate psychoanalytic treatment even though they give no significant place to phallos. Examples: The analyst is deemed to be correct in his or her judgments. The experience of analysands and their connection with the unconscious count for less than the analyst's assessment of the situation. The current outbreak of ethics committees in analytic societies is a response to the unsettling emergence of phallos within the consulting room; phallos will be present in the deliberations even though not given conscious entry. Recent preoccupations with "frame" issues in Jungian circles reflect a failure of nerve relative to the unconscious, a regression into patriarchal technique.

There is more to the matter than psychotherapy. Theodor Reik, the eminent Freudian psychoanalyst, made the following admonition: "The future will show that the use of analysis in the treatment of individual neuroses is not its most important application."[1] He referred to psychoanalysis as the foundation for a new understanding of human nature. Reik suggested a reconnection of psychology with philosophy, whence it emerged as a social and medical science at the end of the nineteenth century. Philosophical inquiry, the investigation of the causes and laws underlying reality, is an inevitable outgrowth of the work of both Freud and Jung and the secular recognition of the unconscious, the underlying stratum of psychic reality. Epistemology, the branch of philosophy having to do with the process of knowing, has been radically altered by the inclusion of subjective, intrapsychic experience as equal in importance to objective empirical data.

Psychoanalytic treatment is inevitably based upon philosophical and epistemological assumptions regarding human nature. Where masculinity and phallos stand, or do not stand, in an analyst's value system is of crucial significance to the analysand, whether male or female. Phallos is always present in psychoanalysis as it is in life. If archetypal phallos is overlooked, it must find a way to enter the process unconsciously. If archetypal phallos is acknowledged and becomes a part of the analytic process, it promises the new knowledge to which Reik referred.

This study is necessarily personal. The reader will discover soon enough that phallos, for me, is an existential god-image. I tried to write psychologically without a personal component integrated into the writing. I failed. As a consequence, I have been taken into places I would rather avoid, as Jung warned. If readers are put off by personal material, let them remember that psychoanalysis is more art than science. Psychology is the discipline of soul, and soul is always a vision of the personal.

"On a visit to the Dordogne area of France in 1986, in the cave Les Combarelles near Les Eyzies, where there are wall engravings dating back to 15,000 B.C., the guide pointed out a vulva, very small, beside the animal carvings. I asked her if there was a masculine sign. She moved her flashlight about four inches to the left, and there was a phallos . . . "
(Author's sketch and notes)

Stone phallos, two feet high, 1st cent. A.D.
(From Pompeii; National Museum, Naples)

1

Phallos and Religious Experience

Phallos as God-Image

As a child of about seven, in the early days of the psychosexual period which Freud called latency, I crawled into my parents' bed one summer morning. We had moved to our summer cottage on White Bear Lake, now a suburb of St. Paul but then two hours' journey by back roads from the city. Mother had left the bed to prepare breakfast. Father lay there asleep, naked. I went under the covers to explore. I may have had a flashlight with me, which would indicate an intention to investigate. Or, sensing there was a discovery to be made, I left the darkness of the blankets to find one. In any case, crouched in the darkness next to my father's body, I came upon his genitalia. I focused the light and gazed upon a mystery. How long I remained there I have no idea; the particulars of the experience have faded. There were no words, then or afterward. As far as I know, my father was not aware that I was there.

What I do remember is the powerful effect the incident had upon me. I think now that I looked upon my father's maleness as a revelation. Certainly at the time I could not articulate what it was; I have difficulty doing that even now. I do know that maleness was unequivocally present before me. There, in those organs, was a picture I had not known before. The picture intimated another world. It was a world I somehow knew existed but until that exposure I had no tangible image to embody my fledgling inner sense. Suddenly, in those naked parts, it faced me.

The other world surely was the potential within me for a sexual life of my own in the future, then only dimly perceived. I also think it was much more. It was the beginning of transpersonal awareness, presented to me as connected with masculine sexual organs. The organs were my father's, and through them I came into being. They were also archetypal in essence—something more, even, than my father. He and I were united within a masculine identity having its roots beyond us both.

My relationship to my father in subsequent years was one of guarded, arm's-length closeness. As I grow older, I discover increas-

13

ingly that I am much like him, more so than I thought possible in earlier years. I catch glimpses of him occasionally, out of the corner of my eye, as I see my reflection in a shop window. When I shave, I sometimes think for a moment that I see him looking at me in the mirror. My smoking habit is certainly his, and I am beginning to hunch over as he did, a telltale sign of his emphysema. I laugh at odd times as he did; I worry about money as he did. Often I think that I am as afraid of my feelings as he was, even after my years of psychoanalysis. I am indebted to him in many ways, not the least being his presence for me on that morning in that bed. He gave me something he did not know he was giving. He had no way of knowing how much I needed it; even if he had, there is no way to give such an experience. It happens. In many ways, that initial exposure of my father's sex was a paradigm of our relationship through the years. What I learned by observing him had less to do with him as a person than with my amazing discovery, and with my search through the fifty years since then for an understanding of what I experienced on that morning.

George Elder of Hunter College writes:

> Phallus, like all great religious symbols, points to a mysterious divine reality that *cannot be apprehended otherwise*. [Emphasis mine] In this case, however, the mystery seems to surround the symbol itself. . . . It is not as a flaccid member that this symbol is . . . important to religion, but as an erect organ.[2]

Carl Jung understood psyche in the original Greek sense of soul, that part of human experience which comes to one from within. Psyche is entwined in mystery and enriched by nuance and meaning, constantly interacting with the outer world but in no sense an epiphenomenon of it. Jung understood religion, generally, as an activity of psyche sui generis, irreducible to any other explanation. He held to this conviction in the face of ridicule and rejection, inevitably cutting himself off from the mainstream of psychoanalysis. By so doing, he made it possible for me to have the tools needed to investigate my experience in my father's bed. Chances are that without Jung and his perspective on psyche, I would be trapped by my experience, bereft of images and a world-view within which to place it. As it is, when I mention to people that I am interested in the sacred nature of phallos, they tend to smile benignly and change the subject.

People are uneasy with the correlation of sexuality and religion. Christianity, especially, has separated the two in a way that would make them appear to be irreconcilable. Psychiatry continues the disjuncture, emphasizing it with pathological labels. The church elevates religion, devaluing sexuality. Psychiatry does the opposite— elevating sexuality and devaluing religion. The union of sexuality and religion is like an electrical connection. Wrong joining leads to disaster. No joining produces no energy. Proper joining holds promise.

Jung is to be celebrated because he held to his conviction that the invisible soul is at least as important a psychological phenomenon as the visible ego—which can be seen, measured and superficially changed. Jung understood that soul is an individual's entrée to a realm of psyche that is universal and eternal, transcending the finite limitations of the ego. He held that psychology is the study of the soul and the discipline of its care. This cannot be done without the inclusion of a world other than that of the ego.

In what sense might my experience in my father's bed be called a religious experience, an encounter with soul? It is a difficult question to answer head-on.

Recently a young man, much in love with the woman he had dated for four years, came into my office. His fiancée had called off their wedding just days before it was to take place. He feared family pressure had been put on her; he felt rejected, abandoned, angry and hurt. Above all, hurt. I saw that his masculine pride was damaged. He was handsome, basically confident, well positioned to make something of himself educationally and professionally, sure of his desire for the woman, almost precocious in his possession of himself. Left fatherless at an early age, he had fathered himself. His hurt was a wounding of soul. The potential loss of his sweetheart was a strongly emotional sting to him. But his hurt was also related to a threatened loss of his self-respect, a questioning of his manhood, a challenge to his sense of direction. These qualities are intrinsically related to phallos. Young or old, males suffer when their phallic identity is threatened.

One can understand this as castration anxiety. That is one way of speaking about what I observed, but it only partly tells the story. Nuance and mystery are gone when one speaks clinically, diagnostically, of castration anxiety. Why is the diminishment of one's masculinity equated with the loss of the male sex organ, while the attainment of manhood is equated with its active use? This question brings one closer to the revelatory quality of phallos. Psyche emerges: phallos carries the masculine inner god-image for a male. The young man was experiencing a threat to this god-image when he felt hurt at the loss of his self-respect. Damage to phallos was at the bottom of his suffering.

This is what Elder means when he refers to phallos as "a mysterious divine reality that cannot be apprehended otherwise." In his intimate relationship with his fiancée the young man knew her generosity, her love, her giving nature. Intimacy was his way of comprehending the feminine, in his partner and in himself (his anima, to use Jung's word). And it was more. His inner reality as a man was tied to the relationship; it informed the young man's sense of who he was. The problem was not only the loss of his woman. Loss of masculine identity was also at stake. Such a loss—or gain as I experienced with my father—is a religious experience, as Jung used the term. It is the crushing of soul or the making of soul as psyche, the invisible reality that supports and gives meaning to existence.

In other words, as phallos enters a situation, an apprehension of masculine divinity takes place that could not take place without phallos. That is the horror of castration. It has always been so. The young man did not consciously create his passion for his fiancée, any more than I created the revelation in my father's bed. Both were visitations. Phallic visitations come as surprise, as grace, time after time, generation after generation, in much the same way, in all cultures. Jung felt that archetypal patterns have coalesced in the psyche through just such constant and similar repetition. Phallos became, over eons of masculine identification with its inner-directed comings and goings, its outer success and defeat, the god-symbol for males. I was able to connect with the young man because I too have felt the devastation of phallic loss. I was able to stay with him because I have also known the glory of phallic resurrection.

Phallic resurrection has to do with the capacity of the male member to return to life, time and again, after defeat and death. Each time phallos explodes in orgasm, it dies. Energy pours forth from phallos as the fountain of life in great excitement, and its time is over. A man is spent. Quiet returns, a desire for rest falls upon a man as though he were falling into the grave—his need for sleep. As Elder points out, phallos is erection, not flaccid penis. Physical phallos has become a religious and psychological symbol because it decides on its own, independent of its owner's ego decision, when and with whom it wants to spring into action. It is thus an appropriate metaphor for the unconscious itself, and specifically the masculine mode of the unconscious.

Penis is phallos *in potentia,* whether or not it is apparent outwardly. In both the interchange with the young man in my consulting room, and my experience with my father, phallic potential was present, though phallos was not. I can imagine saying to myself then, "So this is what I will look like when I am a man. Not only will I grow tall, but all of this will grow too." I can imagine it now because within me still is the seven-year-old boy who wonders at the drawing back of that curtain.

This is religious experience, viewed from the standpoint of psychology. An experience that is also a revelation—such as my childhood discovery, or the young man's trauma in love—permanently affects one's life. If it does not do this, it is not religious. What we take for granted is secular—common, without much meaning, without numinosity, without thrall. The potential for numinosity might be present, but depth is not experienced. That is the case when one merely urinates with his penis, oblivious to the storehouse of energy in one's hand, the cosmic tool, the great sword of heroism. In the course of growing into young adulthood, my experience was forgotten as I went about my boyish business. A functioning ego acts to obstruct awareness of early religious experience so that the grass can be mowed and the arithmetic done. But religious experience returns in the dead of night, between the fine crazing in one's ego-pottery, in intimations and erotic tugs, when one least expects an intrusion. Then one knows that a god is sneaking in, its presence first hinted at in early years.

In the ensuing years I resisted accepting my childhood revelation as a manifestation of the masculine god-image. Phallos was repressed in the cultural structures of my socialization—schooling, good citizenship, profession. In that world, there is no place for phallos as god-image; it is not permitted to participate in everyday life. Physical phallos is acknowledged in asides—in the secrecy of motel rooms and pornography stands, in joking with the boys, in endless fantasies and in the gay world—but furtively, under cover of darkness. Nowhere is phallos out in the open; it sneaks in, since we are embarrassed by its presence. In my early experience, the cover of blankets, the dim light and the unconscious quality of the encounter were paradigmatic.

Men hide their source of authority and power, not exposing their sexuality, their genitalia, in a way similar to the cultural evasion of phallos as god-image. Men substitute phallic surrogates for the thing in itself—family authority, job superiority, institutional construction, female ownership, physical prowess, wealth, religion, politics, intellect and social conformity. This may be a way of protecting the god, as if the inhibition of direct exposure were a way of avoiding an invasion of the sacred tabernacle and diminishing seminal potential. The physiological phenomenon of the drawing of the testes closer to the trunk of the body in time of danger mirrors psychological protective tendencies. The god is revered in the collusion of male secrecy. Men know something they do not speak about directly. They laugh about it together, they implicitly understand one another, but they do not speak openly. A world of mutual knowledge is shared by males without any explicit effort to communicate what is known. Here also one gets close to the religious quality of phallos and to the depths from which it emerges into masculine life. Men have no way to speak about that which is simultaneously known and unknown.

Males expose their phallic member in private, when they are comfortable with their capacity for prowess, when the secret can be shared with another person in intimacy, or when they permit themselves to acknowledge potency alone. They do it when the power of the secret is too strong for containment, when the god demands expression. Men are naked together only within a mutually understood masculine frame of reference, as in athletic shower rooms. Even then, men are careful not to expose phallos. A conflict ensues. Males have genitalia outside the trunk of the body, difficult to hide. Phallos by nature is extraverted, while female organs are introverted. Phallos is external; it desires to show itself in an outward, even blatant way. Phallos stands up, as if to be noticed. A way is required to deal with the doublebind: the need to hide what demands to be exposed. Masculine surrogate behavior and constructions, as mentioned above, serve to resolve the conflict. In modern Western societies, however, males must stumble into an accomplishment of this by themselves. Cultural awareness of the importance of phallos is so low that adequate means are not provided for young men to find a way into adult manhood. There is a male desire for participation in brotherhood—masculine veneration of the god—but hardly any way to attain it. Initiation does not take place. The result, often, is exaggerated exposition or exaggerated protection.

Twenty-five years ago, just after my marriage, I was sent to Uganda by the Episcopal Church to teach for a semester in a theological college near Mbale. The students of the college were males preparing for ordination to the priesthood. All but two had undergone the ritual of circumcision in their native tribes some years before, in early adolescence. In Uganda at the time, male circumcision was cause for great tribal celebration. Ritual circumcision was the manner in which a boy became a man, and it was necessary that the young male undergo the ordeal without flinching or drawing back. The two uncircumcised males in our student body at Buwalasi were different from the others. They may have been the only two that were not married, and they were distinctly inferior to the others in stamina, demeanor and in masculine presence. One of the two had been absent when his time came to be circumcised because his distant grandmother had died. No matter—he had missed his date, and his life was changed. He was not a man.

Male initiation rituals do sneak through in spite of modern ignorance of their importance. In my case, in addition to my fortuitous exposure to my father's maleness, there was membership in a close-knit Boy Scout troop which had use of an isolated and undeveloped campground on a northern Minnesota river. Each boy was ritualistically taken to a country cemetery at night, stripped bare and deserted. He was required to find his way back to the campground, perhaps a mile distant, through the forest. Clearly he could not ask for directions should he come across a farmhouse or a chance car on the road. Eventually such ordeals were stopped, as fraternity hazings have been; for good reason, perhaps, but their purpose is not being served in other ways. The problem is not easy to solve. It is clear, nonetheless, that phallos abhors a vacuum.

For me, the conflict between inner god and outer society as regards phallos finally came to this: either I took seriously the importance of that revelatory experience in my father's bed or admitted to myself that my acceptance of the reality of the unconscious was inadequate. Avoidance of the phallic god-image was avoidance of the unconscious in the service of ego adaptation. The unconscious was offering and phallos was demanding. I was forced to the conclusion that phallos is wondrous and at the same time very odd as a taskmaster. That is what religious people have always said about gods.

Religio and Reductive Analysis

Jung suggested that the Latin *religio* originally came from *religere,* meaning "to go through again, to think over, to recollect." He stated that the church fathers derived *religio* from *religare,* "to reconnect, link back."[3]

Recollection and linking back connect religion with psycho-analysis, the discipline of retrieving forgotten and repressed personal experiences. Jung, with his interest in the collective unconscious, meant by *religio* much more than a recovery of personal moments in time and the effect they had upon a person's present difficulties. Jung wanted to facilitate an existential relationship with that which is beyond ego—with the Self, as he called the central ordering archetype of the psyche. Recollection, in this sense, is generic rather than specifically personal. It is Socratic: drawing out of a person what is inherent in his or her psychic constitution. This is why Jung was concerned about a person's myth. Myth is the language of archetypal inheritance. It is not recommended that one actively seek out the unconscious in younger years. Then, one has experiences, as I did in my father's bed, and goes on. One reconnects later, when perspective and a surfeit of experience bring on reflective possibility. Waves of recollection move in upon one.

Psychoanalytically, one might posit a number of explanations for a revelatory experience. A reductive explanation—referring to nothing beyond the dynamics of personal experience—is faulted by the exclusion of images in the unconscious. The presence or absence of an archetypal god-image can never be fully understood reductively, that is, as a factor only of personal history. Elder's claim that the image of phallos "points to a mysterious divine reality that cannot be apprehended otherwise" stands as a pivotal statement. Elder indicates that phallos, in this instance, functions archetypally, with its own energy. It requires attention regardless of the particular circumstances in which it manifests itself. Elder states that "the mystery seems to surround the symbol itself." This indicates that the symbol has an importance prior to the circumstances of its manifestation. It cannot emerge without a life situation providing a means of entry, but the archetype, not the situation, is the issue

Erect phalli on Island of Delos, Greece (3rd cent. B.C.)

here. Similarly, archetypal phallos stands behind physical phallos as physical phallos stands behind the delivery of semen in sexual intercourse. Jung's concern about genuine symbols has point: symbol *is,* it indicates a reality that cannot be known in any other way. Otherwise, it is not symbol.

To connect back, to go through again, has to do with the presence of power in the original experience. For this reason, psychoanalysts take analysands backward, into abreaction of past trauma. The situation must be relived to undo the fixation. If the original experience were archetypal, however, returning to the image stands on its own as a revelation of psyche, not simply indicating a fixation, a stoppage of development. In point of fact, lack of awareness of the revelation is itself a stoppage of development. Everything depends upon "the back" to which one connects. To explain an archetypal revelation reductively, in terms of a particular life situation—however much the emergence of the archetypal image depends upon that life situation—is tantamount to treating it as nonarchetypal, a mundane occurrence lacking transpersonal power. This is the psychological equivalent of the Christian sin against the Holy Ghost.

The Autonomy of Phallos

Our English word autonomous comes from a combination of the Greek *autos* (self) and *nomos* (law). That which is autonomous is governed by its own law or inner nature.

The importance of autonomy in religion is the experienced fact that the transpersonal dimension of the psyche breaks into the ego at the most inconvenient and surprising of times. Just as we think that things are going well and life is basically under our control, something happens to remind us that this is not true at all. If one were a leaf, floating on the breeze, the breeze would have more to do with where one lands than the intention of the leaf, its color, its structure and its priority of birth on the branch of the tree. Autonomy with regard to phallos is grounded in the experienced reality of men that they cannot, however much they might wish otherwise, make phallos obey the ego. Phallos has a mind of its own. Phallos and the transpersonal have autonomy in common.

An old friend of mine, a Methodist who did not play easily with sexual joking, told me this riddle with glee: "Question: What is a soldier? Answer: A hard cock with a man at the end of it." Other ways of stating the same folk-truth have been mentioned in workshops I have given on masculinity: "What does one do with a cock that will not stop talking?" "A man always thinks through his cock."

A man once told me that he was often impotent with his long-time partner. No matter what he tried at such times, his penis would not transform into phallos. One day he took a young woman out for a drink. They spent time talking about one another and things that concerned them. As he spoke, phallos was there under the table, poised and ready for action. What he could not produce by will power with his partner was present, unbidden, with this young friend. He was perplexed, as men usually are when such a thing happens. He wanted it the other way, but phallos, in its autonomy, denied him. His body (Arnold Mindell would say his "dreambody")[4] spoke against his ego's intention.

A man must realize that this happens and that it pertains to his phallic nature. It may not be what his ego wants to happen, but loyalty to one's mate has no bearing on the autonomous stirrings of phallos, however much it might inhibit a man's sexual behavior. Men come into analytic offices worried that there is something wrong with them because their phallic impulses suggest behavior that is contrary to what they think is right and proper. But of course! Phallos is not governed by the ego or superego, though phallic action certainly can be. Phallic behavior can be restrained by the requirements of civilization. That is a point that will be addressed later in this work. At this juncture, the issue is phallic autonomy and its intrinsic similarity to the autonomy of the unconscious. That is where the religious significance of phallos stands or falls, if the reader will excuse a pun.

Jung wrote in his preface to the second edition of "The Relations between the Ego and the Unconscious":

> I mention these facts because I wish to place it on record that the present essay is not making its first appearance, but is rather the expression of a longstanding endeavour to grasp and—at least in its essential features—to depict the strange character and course of that *drame intérieur*, the transformation process of the unconscious psyche. This idea of *the independence of the unconscious,* which distinguishes my views so radically from those of Freud, came to me as far back as 1902.[5] (Emphasis mine)

Jung used "autonomous" and "independence" interchangeably in his description of the unconscious psyche. Indeed, it was Jung's sense of the mystery and authority of the unconscious, superior to the ego, that radically separated him from Freud in 1914, as the quotation above suggests. (Freud also recognized unconscious superiority, but gnashed his teeth over the matter, and had as his goal the reversal of the condition.) The ego, as conscious man standing before the unknown, responds in fear and trembling to the force of the autonomous unconscious. On a microcosmic level, it is much like the man mentioned above, committed in principle to his partner, suddenly finding phallos present and twitching under the table when with someone else. The discovery hardly left him in fear and trembling . . . although, on second thought, perhaps it did. The portent was enormous. His unexpected phallic reaction to the "sweet young thing" shook his foundations.

To proceed within a wider context of sexuality, it is helpful to consider the contribution of the late Mircea Eliade, noted historian of religion. In *Images and Symbols,* Eliade credits "the surprising popularity of psychoanalysis" with contributing to a new awareness of symbol "regarded as an autonomous mode of cognition."[6] The use of the adjective "autonomous" connects Eliade to Jung's concern about psyche as independent of ego. Eliade discusses sexuality as one such "autonomous mode of cognition." He follows with the momentous statement that sexuality

> everywhere and always . . . is a polyvalent function whose primary and perhaps supreme valency is the cosmological function: so that to translate a psychic situation into sexual terms is by no means to belittle it; for, except in the modern world, *sexuality has everywhere and always been a hierophany,* and the sexual act an integral action and therefore also a means to knowledge.[7] (Emphasis mine)

Sexuality, seen in this light, is a means of experiencing cosmos. Sexuality, as "an autonomous mode of cognition," is a way into the mystery of creation, of approaching and participating in the god-image. Eliade seems to suggest that sexuality is more than *a* way. It may be *the* way. Human beings connect with the deeper aspects of themselves through their sexual, sensual, orgasmic, instinctual experience.

Hierophany means a manifestation of the holy. *Hieros* is sacred in Greek; *phainein* is to show, to make manifest, to clarify. The meaning of sexuality, according to Eliade, is to reveal to human beings that which is beyond ego—in religious terms, the divine. Translated into Jungian terms, sexuality holds within itself a revelation of the archetypal character of the unconscious. Religion is therefore unavoidably concerned with sexuality. Organized religion either encourages a connection with archetypal reality, or it obstructs it. On the one hand, it is good religion; on the other, it is not good. In any case, human beings cannot help but be drawn into the hierophanic process due to their sexual nature, whether or not they consider themselves religious.The great importance all persons place upon sexuality is psychologically grounded in the fact that sexuality is a means of entering and knowing sacred reality. Instinct and archetype are bedfellows, opposite sides of the same coin, as Jung taught. The god-image speaks the language of libido. God, as the Bible teaches, is love.

As mentioned in the introduction, Theodor Reik believed the future would show that "the use of analysis in the treatment of individual neurosis is not its most important application."[8] I would put Reik's prophecy together with Eliade's remarks, in the sense that a deeper and more generally human understanding of symbol, including sexuality as symbol, will broaden and deepen humanity's understanding of itself, and of the enormous forces which live in the unconscious. Psychotherapy is a way of introducing the hierophanic meaning of sexuality to persons who have only a partial notion of what they do with their sexuality, and then only when psychotherapy is sought as a means of self-knowledge and not simply for relief of symptoms. The religious implications of Jung's concept of the unconscious have hardly begun to be applied to psychoanalytic practice some sixty years after his basic texts were written.

Numinosum, Fascinum, **Thrall**

Jung's concept of the supraordinate Self, designating "the whole range of psychic phenomena in man,"[9] draws upon the work of the German theologian Rudolf Otto. Otto's book *Das Heilige* (in English, *The Idea of the Holy*) first appeared in 1917, when Otto was a professor in Marburg. Otto's purpose was to establish an experiential, as opposed to a rational or dogmatic, understanding of religion, and this is what endeared him to Jung.

Otto describes an authentic experience of the holy as *numinous,* conveying to the subject direct knowledge of supernatural divine power. He spoke of a numinous experience as a "unique apprehension of a Something, whose character may at first seem to have little connection with our ordinary moral terms, but later 'becomes charged' with the highest and deepest moral significance."[10] The term moral, for Otto, did not refer to an ethical process but to the "Something" having psychological rather than tangible effects. One can substitute psychological for moral in the above statement. Otto's words describe my experience in my father's bed, if the "Something" is understood to be my perception of phallos.

For Otto, the mental state of perceiving the numinous is "perfectly *sui generis* and irreducible to any other."[11] Otto's grasp of the extraordinary subjective quality in an experience of the *numen* (called by Otto's translator "the most general Latin word for supernatural divine power")[12] was useful to Jung as he sought to make clear the marks of a personal experience of the Self. The issue continues to be important. Jung sought a way to express how the appearance of a god-image might be a manifestation of the Self and therefore psychologically valid rather than pathological. Furthermore, if Jung were to go beyond Freud's reductive method in understanding psyche, he needed a language that psychology could not then provide. Otto's terminology helped Jung to explain an outside-of-the-ego perception and the emotional response evoked in a person by such a perception.

Jung borrowed from Otto the term *mysterium tremendum* to express a subjective experience of the *numen,* which Otto said produced personal reactions of awe, overpoweredness, the influx of energy, an awareness of the presence of the "wholly other," and fascination.[13] Jung knew these to be human responses to the presence of a god-image, a symbol of the Self. Jung understood that every archetype is essentially beyond representation. One senses the presence of an archetype through an image (mental, sensory or affective) and, even more essentially, in the strength of the emotional response which the image induces in the receiver. Understanding phallos as a numinous god-image is aided by the work of Otto and Jung.

One response to a numinous presence Otto identifies as fascination. Thomas Wright, in his 1866 essay, "A Worship of the Generative Powers," claims that "one name of the male organ among the Romans was *fascinum* . . . hence [is] derived the words to fascinate and fascination."[14] Jung wrote of the human response to an image of the Self in terms such as *fascinosum* and *numinosum,* but as far as I know he never made a connection between *fascinum* and phallos. He did, however, make the remarkable statement that "phallus is the source of life and libido, the creator and worker of miracles, and as such it was worshipped everywhere."[15]

Phallos as an object of fascination has to do with its capacity to charm, which is the root meaning of the Latin *fascio.* To return once again to the opening vignette of this chapter, my response to the unveiling of phallos in my father's bed was one of fascination. Charm is elemental curiosity, drawing power, a magical capacity to move one from the ordinary to the numinous—the characteristics of a religious experience. For instance, an analysand spoke of his response to the obelisk on a recent trip to Egypt: "I could not take my eyes from it"—an experience which repeated itself upon each encounter. Fascination is an engagement of soul; it is the experience of a symbol's capacity to charm, to seize one emotionally, to make known a hidden power.

When such an experience occurs, there often comes another response which can be called thrall. Thrall is a nicely anachronistic word and highly emotional in tone; in current usage it suggests a feminine captivation by phallos. Riveting one's attention might be a less ornate way of speaking of thrall, but it contains little of the devotion that thrall connotes. Men tend to repress this aspect of their interest in phallos and to be uncomfortable with it, disliking it in themselves and in other men. Thrall suggests servitude, bondage, worship. Men think these responses to phallos are appropriate, even desirable, for women, but god forbid, not for themselves. Men *are* phallos, after all. One does not worship what one is.

Dignified diffidence toward phallos is an ego attitude and in no way circumscribes the actual psychological situation for men. Men can be as enthralled with phallos as women, perhaps even more so since the cultural prohibitions against it are so strong. In point of fact, human beings do worship what they are; they can bind themselves to idealized versions of human attributes; they can serve gods who link human qualities with images from the unconscious. The *numinosum* intrudes into one's life where and when it finds an opportunity, ego be damned. This is a factor in the common experience of married men who are surprised by phallic thrall in mid-life and suspect, with terror, that they have a homosexual component. Whether this means that a man is gay is a moot point. It does indicate an archetypal and numinous phallic presence lying beneath consciousness, stronger and more fascinating to some persons than to others, but not cause for hysterical alarm. Phallic thrall is a symptom of masculine hierophany. It can be worked into one's life as Jesus thrall can be, or even Jung thrall, without the train necessarily leaving the tracks.

Terracotta lamp, eight inches high, 1st cent. A.D.
(From Pompeii; National Museum, Naples)

2

Archetypal Phallos

Phallic Worship

This is not the place for a survey of the ancient manifestations of phallic worship, although historic antecedents are helpful in understanding phallos as a god-image. For the serious student, there are resources. Among these are Alexander Stone's *The Story of Phallicism* (1927) and two essays—one by Richard Payne Knight, "A Discourse on the Worship of Priapus" (1786), the other by Thomas Wright, "A Worship of the Generative Powers" (1866)—reprinted together in a volume called *Sexual Symbolism*.

Collective, explicit phallic worship is virtually nonexistent among Western people. It is not a present reality anywhere in the world save among certain Hindu believers in India, where Shiva as *lingam* (phallos) is outwardly acknowledged as an image of divinity. Shivaism, today a cult within modern Hinduism, is, according to Alain Daniélou, the oldest religion, having originated during the Neolithic age (10,000–8,000 B.C.) among the Dravidian peoples of what is now India, and carried by them to the Mediterranean. There it became the basis of Greek Dionysianism. Shiva's symbol, the *lingam,* or phallos, Daniélou calls

> the mysterious organ by which the creative principle is visibly represented . . . [containing] the sperm, which potentially contains the whole of ancestral and racial heritage and the genetic characteristics of the future human being . . . the organ through which a link is established between man (or animal or flower) and the creative force which is the nature of the divine. It is the most perfect example of a symbol.[16]

> Shiva said,
> I am not distinct from the phallos.
> The phallos is identical with me.
> It draws my faithful to me
> And therefore must be worshipped.
> Wherever there is an upright male organ,
> I, myself, am present, even if there is no other representation
> of me.[17]

29

The teaching of the *Linga Purana* continues:

> The basis of the entire world is phallos.
> Everything is born of the *Linga*.
> He who desires perfection of soul must worship the *Linga*.[18]

The teaching of the *Shiva Purana, Vidyeshvara Samhita* continues: "It is the symbol of the origin of all things. / The phallos is . . . the symbol of the god."[19]

Here is the reason for thrall, and not only for females. The *lingam* is worshiped by Shivaite Hindus in India in the form of an upright stone or an ithyphallic (erect) image of the god, and in Shivaite temples the *lingam* is represented as inserted in the *yoni,* a circular stone representing the female organ. Daniélou states that the *lingam* appears often in the form of a pillar, "as found almost everywhere in the world."[20]

The statement above is reminiscent of Jung's important yet almost inexplicable statement, mentioned in the previous chapter, that "phallus is the source of life and libido, the creator and worker of miracles, and as such, it was worshipped everywhere."[21] Jung's comment is strange because it is an aside in a general discussion of psychic energy, and the specific reference to phallos as "worshipped everywhere" is unsupported. The statement is, none the less, completely congruent with a Shivaistic understanding of the importance of phallos as the visual manifestation of masculine creative energy raised to a sacred level.

Phallic worship as an historical phenomenon and phallos as psychological god-image are not the same. They are related to one another but not necessarily dependent upon one another. Jung's statement that phallos is worshiped everywhere is a psychological declaration, not one of historic fact in a collective sense. My brief presentation of Hindu Shiva is meant to serve as a demonstration of the power of phallos emerging fully within a religious culture, and as an indication of interpretive direction when one approaches phallos from a psychological perspective. A once-extant, pervasive Shivaic phallic divinity has disappeared from the surface of Western life. It is a certainty that phallos has moved into the realm of the unconscious, where its influence is no less pervasive.

Let us recall at this point that Jung differed from Freud significantly in his concept of the structure of the unconscious. For both Freud and Jung, the unconscious was divided into two conceptual parts.

Lingam in *yoni,* union of masculine and feminine.
(Pitt Rivers Museum, Oxford, England)

Freud was somewhat less clear in their demarcation than was Jung. For Freud, that which was present in a person's psychic field but out of the range of one's consciousness was the unconscious. The first part was the forgotten and repressed memories of one's past life; the second part, the id, was instinctual, the inheritance of the race, dominated by sexuality and self-denial. Jung called the first of these—the forgotten and/or repressed memories of one's historic life—the personal unconscious. What Freud called the id Jung included in the collective unconscious. Freud paid attention, mostly, to what Jung called the personal unconscious, the effect of a person's past on a person's present. Jung paid attention, mostly, to the instinctual patterns in the psyche which cause human beings, generally, to think, feel and behave as they do.

For Jung, the collective unconscious became a more developed concept than Freud's id. "More developed" is an understatement. Jung's inclusion of Freud's id, important as that was, was but the starting point of his investigations and theorizing about the vast substratum of the psyche. Central, structurally, in the collective unconscious (which Jung also called the objective psyche) are the archetypes, or typical models after which similar things are patterned, in the Platonic sense of the idea or ideal. Jung felt that archetypal patterns determine the way behavior emerges in animal and human life and images appear in the consciousness of human beings. Archetypal patterning is not learned. The patterns are similar in kind to instincts (Freud's id) and are universal among the world's races and peoples, however different may be the cultural peculiarities among them. In this sense, they are transpersonal: the patterns are universal, not limited to a personal connection with the archetype.

Archetypes produce images which the mind and the body receive. Phallos is such an image. Phallos is an archetypal image in that it is a universal attribute of maleness which has a similar valence or meaning everywhere. It is not rediscovered or relearned with each new male birth. Phallic patterning is imbedded in the psyche at its deepest level and as such it is as innate as maleness itself. A male inherits archetypal phallic characteristics even as he inherits his penis. As a man's penis is characteristically his own, so his phallic archetypal pattern is individual to him. While each man's image reception is somewhat different from his neighbor's, yet phallos is recognizably similar in pattern and easily distinguishable from that which is not phallic.

In the remainder of this chapter, I present three examples of archetypal phallic images which have directly affected my life as an adult, images with which I have had important personal contact and about which I can write with an intensity and intimacy that is personally religious. Each of these examples, in its own way, involves worship, autonomy, fascination and numinosity in my subjective experience of an objective archetypal image.

A Transpersonal Phallic Dream

In 1968 I had been vicar of St. Clement's Church in New York City for three years. St. Clement's was an unusual Episcopal church in almost every way, a kind of wonderful precocious child of the sixties. Except for the Eucharist on Sunday, it was a theater. The presence of theater in the liturgical space made it possible to experiment with worship, gradually to eliminate certain customs which interfered with wholesome communication, to hear "the word" as it came from sources other than those traditionally understood to be religious. The congregation was transitional and transitory, highly intelligent and artistic, and strongly given to press against the boundaries of convention and authority. There was a great deal of political unrest, and more searching than conviction. Each Sunday morning was like an opening night; one never quite knew what might happen. Furthermore, St. Clement's was good press copy, and we were covered incessantly by the media.

The pressure on me, as the vicar, was enormous. I was both ready and not ready for such an assignment. I had to grow into it. I was expected to be the leader of the congregation, and I expected this of myself, but I was not sure how to lead when there were increasingly few anchoring points. My political and theological views had been rather conservative and were in the throes of changing. I was not adrift, but I was nervous and at times unsure of myself. As often as not, the congregation was leading me.

At that time I was working analytically with Esther Harding, the first Jungian analyst in the United States. She was an elderly and rather delicate-appearing maiden lady, the daughter of an English vicar. I brought to her my dream of a great phallos appearing in a circle of naked men who were lying on the ground. Each man had his feet placed upon the base of the phallos, and each had his hand upon his neighbor's erect member. Dr. Harding asked about the central image: "Was it a man's phallos?" "Certainly not," I replied, "it was much too big for that." "Was it a giant's phallos?" she asked. "No, it was much too big even for that." "Well, then, Mr. Monick, *whose* do you think it was?"

The implication was that it was for me a god-image, even a symbol of the Self. I remember that she was amused by her line of questioning, and by my surprise. I remember that I was bemused by the possibility of a phallos being as strong a presence as divinity. As a Christian priest, I was not at ease with a phallic god-image, St. Clement's or no St. Clement's. I had nowhere to put such a suggestion, no way to incorporate it in my life.

Psychology as the science of the soul has as a major concern the hidden inner person, the center of which is the Self, as Jung called it. Jung chose the name Self for the central archetype of the psyche because the term connects, in a radical way, the *mysterium tremendum* (in Otto's words) with the personal experience of the perceiving ego. In English, one is used to referring to oneself (as ego) as "myself." Such a use of language misses Jung's point, if ever so slightly. "Myself" is a combination of two words—"my," indicating ego, and "self," indicating a central supraordinate personality. English, then, does indicate, in a way, Jung's perception of the Self, although few English-speaking persons are aware of the confession they make when using the term.

Dream images such as the one mentioned above have an effect upon the dreamer whether or not the dreamer is aware of that effect. Dreams function much like other "given" psychological or physiological phenomena. If I drive down a steep hill at a rapid clip and there is a sharp curve in the road at the bottom, my car must negotiate the curve or end up in the ditch. The presence of the curve is not dependent upon my awareness of it. What matters is that I am aware of the impending danger and that I govern my car accordingly.

My dream was a gift from the unconscious at a time of experienced need. The dream presented to me an image of masculine presence and stability, of authority and virility, when my ego was at its limits, when I required help. Jung states, time and again, that it is at such times that the Self makes its presence felt—Christians would call it an act of grace. But why phallos? Presumably because my conscious ego required such an image to give it substance. In this instance, it enabled me to stand up, as phallos stands up, perhaps faulted in its performance from time to time, but alive and unquestionably present. It fed courage into me, allowing me to laugh at the nonsense of St. Clement's just when I was taking it so seriously. It placed my ego on a foundation as strong and firm as poised phallos itself. It provided me with the capacity to deliver my seed to the congregation, in a way that was right and natural for me.

The image of men at the base of a phallos, in a mandala formation, with their hands on their neighbors' members, has obvious homosexual overtones. It is of little concern to the unconscious that the suggestion of homosexuality may make a man uncomfortable. If such an image has the capacity to jolt a man awake, to point to a source of strength he had not considered, to instruct in a needed direction, then the image will come, without regard to comfort. Here is an example of the limitation of Freud's notion that the dream protects sleep for the sake of the defense of the ego.

Homosexual urges are often an indication that a man requires an infusion of the masculine in his life. Whether or not he ever acts out this awareness sexually is another matter. The need is focused

Ancient Japanese stone group, archetypally similar to the author's
dream-image of "a great phallos appearing in a circle of naked men
on the ground."

upon phallos in a concrete way, or upon any number of symbolic
phallic expressions that are not ordinarily understood or experienced
to be erotic. Phallos always brings substantiation of masculine
strength. For an insecure male, phallos is almost literally a godsend,
whether phallos appears as itself (as in my dream) or in any number
of kindred forms.

My phallos dream was not primarily erotic. It was an image of
male bonding around an archetypal god-image of maleness. The
men were not making love to one another or involved in erotic play.
Their connection was structural and straightforward, suggesting
something other than eros. Transpersonal phallos—a bigger-than-life
member rising above the men in the circle, a stanchion to which

each is connected by his feet being planted upon it as a "ground," with each man attached to his neighbor by hand and individual phallos in a kind of masculine brotherhood, a mandala of acknowledged phallos carriers—is the central message of the dream. Every man has the capacity for some degree of homosexual interest, every man has a homosexual "radical"—as the Danish psychoanalyst Thorkil Vanggaard calls it.[22] How this appears in any one man is a factor of the masculine/feminine balance in his psyche, the configuration of archetypes in his deep unconscious, his environmental influences, genetic inheritance and the extent to which he has suppressed or repressed his homosexual interest.

Homoeroticism enters the picture when a male's need for masculine affirmation is urgent and his hunger for phallos becomes sexual desire. Three distinct factors are involved. One is the homosexual radical present in all men. Another is the emergence of eroticism based upon this radical and upon need. Still another is the acting out of homoerotic desire in sexual behavior. How and when one of these factors transforms into another is an important question, but beyond the scope of this work. The point emphasized here is that homosexual and homoerotic problems brought by men into psychoanalytic treatment have an archetypal core and should be examined in this light in therapy. Both Eliade and Jung write that sexuality, heterosexual or homosexual, is at bottom a religious issue, opening a door in the psyche which permits the god-image standing behind it an entrance into ego awareness.

The Cerne Giant

A remarkable archetypal image of phallos can be observed in the figure of the Cerne Giant, a 180-foot outline figure carved into the side of a gentle chalk hill near the village of Cerne Abbas in Dorset, a rural county on the south coast of England. The Giant sports an erection which, including the testicles, is some 36 feet in length, or 20% of the entire figure. That is a very large erection. A six-inch erection on a six-foot man amounts to 8% of his body height; 20% of six feet would be 14½ inches, a rare erection indeed (and useless in practice). The Giant's erection is nearly the length of his head. Clearly, such a portrayal has symbolic importance.

In his right hand, the Giant holds a knotted club, raised as if to strike. The left arm is outstretched with a clenched fist, and there

The Cerne Giant.
(From *The Tourist Guide to Dorset*)

are signs that it may have originally carried a cloak, after the fashion of the Greek god Hermes. The British National Trust roadside plaque states that the figure is of Romano-British origin. John Sharkey, in *Celtic Mysteries: The Ancient Religion,* estimates that it was made in the first century B.C.[23]

That such a figure survived the years of Victorian prudery is cause for wonder. But the Cerne Giant, strangely, remains in relative obscurity even today. A good friend, whose mother was born in Dorset, introduced me to the Giant by a postcard he sent me some fifteen years ago. In planning a recent visit to England with my son to celebrate his graduation from college, I inquired about the Giant at the British travel office in New York. No one there had heard of it. (Later I discovered that it is pictured in the official Dorset travel guide!) There are people who have lived in Dorset for fifty years and know nothing of it. This monumental phallic figure is quite obviously repressed as a god-image, or any kind of image for that matter.

One can view the figure from only one place, a small parking area at a turn in the road as one descends into the tiny hamlet of Cerne Abbas from the north. If one's head is not pointed in the direction of the Giant, he is there and gone before one knows it. A shallow valley of about a mile separates the viewer from the figure. It seems obvious that the Giant was not intended to be seen by humans, since the only way he can be adequately viewed is from the air. It was suggested during a recent television presentation on English hill figures that they were made to be seen by the gods. They may have been votive offerings, celebrating attributes of the divinity to which the god's attention was called.

When my son and I came in sight of the Giant, a group of American teenaged bicyclists, male and female, simultaneously happened upon it unawares from the opposite direction. They slammed on their brakes. They could not believe their eyes. The girls held back, as though embarrassed. The boys were excited. They jumped about like Mexican beans, hooting, hollering, slapping each other on the back. Their response was almost as interesting to me as the Giant himself.

The next day my son and I climbed up the hill for a more intimate visit. I made a weak stab at doing what my postcard friend had suggested as a real neolithic thrill—have a picnic in the Giant's left testicle. I climbed over the protective fence and trod upon the outline of phallos and testes. I sat down upon the head of phallos, as women do when they wish to conceive, even today. It was no great shakes but it was interesting. It was a connection with my childhood discovery in my father's bed. It was a connection with my own god-phallos dream, and to Jung's childhood phallic dream (discussed in the next chapter). It was important for me to share this with *my* son, in a more conscious way than my early connection in bed with my father. It was an acknowledgment of the phallic identity which we share, and it suggested the transcendent character of that identity.

I am not sure what it meant to my son. We did not talk about it much. Consciousness may have been raised a cubit in a generation, but it did not reach its zenith. We went on from there to Stonehenge, Salisbury, Wells, Oxford, heroic Glastonbury (where Stephen climbed the phallic Tor), T. S. Eliot's grave in East Coker, Avebury Circle and Wookey Hole, and a visit to an old lady in Mappowder, the last surviving sister of the novelist brothers Powys.

The agenda of the trip was mine. Stephen knew that he was a son being taken on a journey of significance to his father, to show the son what was important to the father, a rite of passage as the son moved into independent manhood.

Despite arguments about driving, about hotels, about too many cathedrals, about the best way to get to the Giant by the back of the overgrown mountain, we held together through what seemed to him, I am sure, a tour-de-force of antiquities. My wife had been mildly suspicious of the trip plan as I conjured it up beforehand. Yet she, the mountain climber, herself worked out dozens of hiking and climbing junkets in New Hampshire and Switzerland in earlier years, dragging us all along. Stephen is now an experienced climber, having conquered Kilimanjaro.

Love is not democracy. We have tried democracy in our family, and it almost always fails. Love is inviting someone into the personal recesses of one's desire. That recess is not always the other person's. A willingness to go along with the fantasy of the other is a sign of requited love, either whole or in part.

Epstein's Saint Michael and the Devil

On that same father-son mini-odyssey, Stephen and I visited Coventry to see the old medieval cathedral, gutted by incendiary bombs during World War Two, and the attached new cathedral, designed by Sir Basil Spence and completed in 1958. In spite of its impressive size and many ingenuities, the modern work was something of a disappointment to me. The raising of a new temple from the ashes of the old is laudable and the product is distinguished. Yet something is missing from the new, something intangible. Spence's new cathedral, even with the herculean Sutherland tapestry over the altar, cannot capture the sense of mystery and authentic spirituality inherent in the old. In the new, the symbolism, if one can call it that, is consciously reinvented, in a day when popular faith in the Christian myth is past its prime.

There was, however, a feature of the new cathedral that took my breath away. On the facade of the new church is mounted Sir Jacob Epstein's metal sculpture of St. Michael, after whom the cathedral is named, and the devil. Michael, the archangel, stands tall, with one arm raised, brandishing a sword—a pose similar to that of the Cerne Giant. Michael is a slim and ethereal youth who has vanquished the devil, lying in chains at his feet. The devil has an altogether different masculine body from Michael, far from boyish. He is depicted as mature, strong, well muscled, not in the least ethereal. Very significant are the genitalia. Michael is swathed in a rippled cloth, covering his midsection. A barely visible protuberance suggests the presence of a penis beneath the cloth. Not so the devil. His naked and realistic penis and testicles, quite apparent in the shadows of his open legs, are ample and swarthy. The devil is clearly depicted as sexual, the opposite of Michael. Michael's spiritual sword has conquered corporeality and psychologically emasculated it.

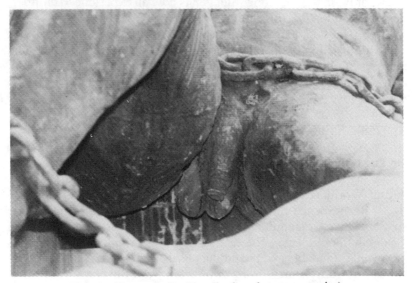

The devil's genitalia (detail of sculpture opposite).

Sir Jacob Epstein's sculpture of St. Michael and the devil.

St. Michael and the devil was precisely the image I needed to illustrate the point of this work. The sculpture depicts St. Paul's viewpoint on sexuality as he wrote to the new Christians of Galatia:

Walk in the Spirit
And ye shall not fulfill the lust of the flesh.
For the flesh lusteth against the Spirit
And the Spirit against the flesh:
And these are contrary the one to the other.[24]

St. Paul is far indeed from Eliade's understanding of sexuality as hierophany. Sexuality, instead of revealing the divine, has become for St. Paul an enemy of the divine. For reasons that I will not go into here, Christianity adopted St. Paul's antipathy to the flesh. That which was sacred had become profane. Epstein's Michael clearly denigrates physicality and sexuality. Masculinity, following St. Paul, should be spiritual only. Phallos, as physical organ, is devilish. Physicality and spirituality are fundamentally opposed. If one wins, the other loses, and in the case of physical phallos it is the will of God that it lose.

Alternative notions of the importance of physical phallos became part of gnostic traditions swept aside by triumphant Christianity, falling into the unconscious of Western civilization. It is for this reason that Jung strongly valued the alchemical and other rejected byways in medieval European culture. There is where devilish phallos lay—covered over and consciously ignored, apparent only in the secrecy of dreams and other closed-off places, and in the behavior of the outcast.

With the modern demise of institutional and doctrinal Christianity and the patriarchy espoused and carried by the Pauline church, phallos is emerging from its hidden gnostic reservoir. It is ironic that a sculpture on a modern Christian church should so dramatically proclaim an understanding of masculine sexuality and body that is held openly as doctrine today only by the most reactionary and repressed Christians.

It will be many years before phallos fully emerges from its catacomb entombment. It will be many years before the devil is seen as a psychological factor in each person—and, according to Jung, in the deity itself[25]—rather than as specific to phallos, sexuality and the flesh. Phallos, of course, participates in evil, as does every facet of the created order. But not as Epstein's sculpture states. Such an image seriously distorts psychological reality.

3

Phallos in Psychoanalysis

In no sense will the material covered in this chapter be a review of the literature on phallos, or phallos-oriented concepts, in psychoanalytic writing. Rather, two remarkable and well-known statements, one by Freud and one by Jung, will be examined as a means of presenting to the reader a general background of the idea of phallos in the minds of the fathers of psychoanalysis. As the reader will see, the concept of the mother is imbedded in each, making it necessary to include a brief treatment of her importance to a consideration of the psychoanalytic understanding of the roots of masculinity.

Freud's "Final" Statement

In the last section of his essay, "Analysis Terminable and Interminable," written in 1937 (shortly before his death in 1939), Freud states:

> Two themes come into especial prominence and give the analyst an unusual amount of trouble. It soon becomes evident that a general principle is at work here. . . . tied to the distinction between the sexes. . . . [and] there is an obvious correspondence between them. . . . The two corresponding themes are in the female, *an envy for the penis*—a positive striving to possess a male genital—and in the male, *a struggle against his passive or feminine attitude toward another male*. [Emphasis mine] What is common to the two themes was singled out at an early date by psycho-analytic nomenclature as an attitude toward the castration complex. . . . I think that, from the start, "repudiation of femininity" would have been the correct description of this remarkable feature in the psychical life of human beings. . . . We often have the impression that with the wish for a penis and the masculine protest we have penetrated through all the psychological strata and have reached *bedrock* [emphasis mine], and that thus our activities are at an end.[26]

Written from the vantage point of half a century of pioneering experience and reflection, these are important words. Freud seems to mean that phallos (penis, to Freud) is so important that all of psychoanalytic work revolves around its presence or absence in a person's life, whether male or female. Fear of the lack or loss of phallos in a male, and absence of and desire for it (penis envy) in a female, constitute the "castration complex." Freud comments that a better description of "this remarkable feature in the psychical life of human beings" might be the "repudiation of femininity." To Freud, the possession of phallos is the same as repudiation of the feminine, and the loss of phallos—experienced on the part of a male defeated by another male, and assumed, psychologically, on the part of the female—is equated with feminization. Without phallos, all is feminine.

It is important to understand the rationale behind this claim. It has to do with the importance of the mother as the experienced source of life and as the nurturer of life prenatally and in early childhood. It has to do, also, with the tendency a human being has to identify with the perceived source of life, the mother, and the initial sense of well-being one needs to experience in her presence. This universal human requirement places the mother in a most powerful position, and she is thus understood in every psychoanalytic school.

In the case of a female, identification with the mother poses no structural problems relative to her sense of herself as a woman. She is of the same nature as her source. In the case of a male, however, a serious problem immediately presents itself. He is not of the same nature as his source. If he is to know this, a fundamental masculine differentiation must take place. The mother may help a male child by her acceptance of his essential difference from herself, or she may hinder the process by binding him to her.

A life-task is thus set out for a male, a task for which phallos is the symbol. It takes varying forms over the course of a man's life. As a child, the boy wants to get out of the house, his mother's domain. (If he does not want to do so, he is likely to be labeled a sissy; his masculinity is in question from the start.) He wants and needs to sass back, to pry himself away, to act rough. Later, the boy misbehaves in more serious ways, gets into trouble, stays out late, begins to close up and be secretive to his mother, no longer "her boy" in the same way. Still later, he begins to shift his interest to girls. This is the natural and usual process, without which masculine development is stunted and infantile identification with the mother continues. Phallos remains the property of the mother who produced it. She is the authority. Castration has begun. This is the feminization process in a male, inimicable to his psychological connection with phallos.

According to Freud, the threat of psychological castration also appears in a male who has his masculine identity more or less intact. Defeat by another male is reminiscent of mother-castration and accentuates the fear of it. Loss, to the male, inevitably implies the loss of phallos—whether the loss be of money, of property, lover, wife, children, position, influence, authority. An identity crisis is likely to result. A man wants relief, reassurance, restoration, all associated with the mother. He wants both the comfort of the mother and the reestablishment of his phallic identity, which is associated with his liberation from her. (Often the situation repeats itself over and over again, usually because separation from the mother has not been accomplished. This is classic *puer aetermus* psychology.)[27]

One cannot go backward and forward simultaneously. If a male embarks on a regressive path, he bears the marks of psychological castration. He remains the son of his mother, or of a mother surrogate, who may be his wife, or, as a reader of this work suggested, his bishop. Often his captor is the actual mother herself, whose dependence upon the son does not serve to anchor his manhood, as one might suppose. Rather, it depletes him, hinders his independence and autonomy, diminishes his ability to function phallically. It is just this connection which poses the threat for a male in an unresolved oedipal love affair with his mother. The male can never rid himself of a fierce and prior inner psychological connection with his original partner; he is the son-lover, psychologically, whose phallic energy is devoured by the commitment.

One can observe the outer manifestations of the mother-son marriage in many ways. There are sons who can hardly make a move without consulting their mothers. There are those who return to their mothers in later days, sometimes from far distant places, when the mother needs protection, when the struggle to stay apart is no longer worth the price that must be paid by the son. There is the final return to the burial place of the mother. There is the patriotic urge to return home, to acknowledge the tie to the motherland, a much stronger and more accurate terminology than fatherland. The mother finally wins. In Scranton, where I live much of the time, the two Sunday papers each display some thirty pages of family portraits on Mother's Day in May, often with four generations of mothers and sons and daughters and their progeny in an open-faced testimony to the power of the mother connection. For a daughter, there is no structural problem in a strong psychological connection with the mother, however debilitating its effect may be upon her animus, her husband, her children. For a son, however, the situation is potentially lethal.

A male's captor may be his wife or lover, whom he dare not but obey. A captured male feels that he is nothing in himself if he has no woman. A form of continuing attachment to the mother is the desire for wealth with its luxurious creature comforts, including the servility to style, aesthetics and importance which come in its wake. Signs of castration, the absence of phallos, are present no matter how many women a man beds or wants to bed.

The man whose masculinity is mother-dominated makes a series of conquests but retreats as soon as the difficult task of supporting woman and child presents itself. Erection, in such an instance, limits itself to genital expression; entering a female is entering a soft place, receptive to phallos. Intercourse can be reentering the comforts of the mother. The test comes in a male's ability to transfer instinctual phallic strength to social phallic purpose, and transfer it again to instinctual phallic strength, knowing, within himself, that each is a reflection of the other, never to be separated.

This cannot be done unless the mother is in some way "abandoned" by the son in favor of an independent phallic thrust and, eventually, phallic responsibility—the building of his own home, becoming head of his own tribe. It was the father's responsibility to take care of the mother in the oedipal situation, pushing the son away, freeing the son to go his own way without a debilitating and castrating responsibility for and to the mother. In such a way does a father, denying his son the comforts of the father's wife, pass on masculinity to his son.

Freud's general principle is the need on the part of a male for a psychological separation from the feminine—its "repudiation." It is quite acceptable as far as it goes. But for an antidote to castration that moves more deeply into the unconscious, one must turn to Jung.

Jung's "First" Dream

Jung wrote in his memoirs, *Memories, Dreams, Reflections,* of the earliest dream he could remember, one that preoccupied him all his life. He was between three and four years old when, in the dream, he discovered a dark, rectangular stone-lined hole in the ground, and descended into it via a stone stairway, fearfully.

> At the bottom was a doorway with a round arch, closed off by a green curtain. It was a big, heavy curtain of worked stuff like brocade, and it looked very sumptuous. Curious to see what might be hidden behind, I pushed it aside. I saw before me in the dim light a rectangular chamber about thirty feet long. The ceiling was arched and of hewn stone. The floor was laid with flagstones, and in the centre a red carpet ran from the entrance to a low platform. On this platform stood a wonderfully rich golden throne. . . . a real king's throne in a fairy tale. Something was standing on it which I thought at first was a tree trunk twelve to fifteen feet high and about one and a half to two feet thick. It was a huge thing, reaching almost to the ceiling. But it was of a curious composition: it was made of skin and naked flesh, and on top there was something like a rounded head with no face and no hair. On the very top of the head was a single eye, gazing motionlessly upwards.
>
> It was fairly light in the room, although there were no windows and no apparent source of light. Above the head, however, was an aura of brightness. The thing did not move, yet I had the feeling that it might at any moment crawl off the throne like a worm and creep towards me. I was paralysed with terror. At that moment I heard from outside and above me my mother's voice! She called out, "Yes, just look at him. That is the man-eater!" . . . I awoke sweating and scared to death.[28]

Jung goes on to say, "Only much later did I realize that what I had seen was a phallus, and it was decades before I understood that it was a ritual phallus. . . . the phallus of this dream seems to be a subterranean God 'not to be named.'"[29]

Jung wrote his autobiography as an octogenarian. Why would he remember that early dream at such a late age, and why would he tell it to the world? Clearly it had something to do with his lifelong preoccupation with that transpersonal phallic image.

Jung's antidote for the basic fear of castration, or being lost in the mother, is found in his central placement of the hero mythologem in the development of masculine psychology and of consciousness.[30] The hero represents not only the developmental process of an individual male, but also, phylogenetically and archetypally, the process of ego development in the history of the species. Ego must separate from its unconscious matrix as boy must separate from mother. As with Freud's model, the hero must go forward, not backward, in the face of the mother-castration challenge and the ordeals resulting from his independence. If he retreats in an essential way he is lost. Strategic retreat may be necessary from time to time but, phallos-like, not abandonment of purpose.

Jung's hero follows Freud's masculine general principle—repudiation of femininity—to an extent: his youthful feminine side must be pushed aside, as well as the mother, with whom his feminine side is identified. The hero accomplishes this through rigorous and risky personal testing: moving out of mother-protection in loyalty to himself; the battle with the mother-dragon; the dreaded and lonely night sea journey, when his inner mettle is honed; the winning of the maiden; progenitoration; husbanding; and aiding the renewal of the king, or perhaps becoming the king himself. Masculinity is an accomplishment, not a birthright—so strong is the pull of nature-mother. But Jung's hero as the mythologem of masculine development emerges from the archetypal realm; phallos initiates, stands behind and furthers the process. Jung's point of view, furthermore, is more holistic than Freud's construct, since the action establishes masculinity per se and not only as "repudiation of the feminine."

In the ideal development of masculinity, these feats are substantially accomplished. The boy becomes the young man who becomes the established man—somewhat more tired of the struggle than in times past, more ready to smoke his pipe and ponder things. Then another transformation begins to take place. The wise old man or senex is called forth when the paunch appears and the hair turns white. Men resist such signs as indications of the end of youthful potency and rush to gymnasiums and hairdressers to rectify the doldrums. Not so fast, gentlemen! Beyond superficial restorations, the change cannot be halted, nor should it be. There is a new pleasure in store for the wiser, older man, and a need for him. He walks more slowly, pointing the way with his phallic cane, knowing and demonstrating the difference between what is important and what is not, between dross and substance. He can be troublesome, but he has earned respect.

The inner quality which prompts and feeds masculine development is phallos. A male knows this because of the importance to him of his masculine organ in its energized, invasive, penetrating mode. Hard phallos is a quality of youth and early manhood, the sign of heroic stance, sword raised high upon silver steed. As age descends upon a man, his hardness changes, becomes less apparent, less the

Molded vase, 6th cent. B.C.
(From Kamirus, Rhodes; British Museum, London)

signature of his body, less urgent to him concretely. Rarely do older men announce to the world their significance in ways so important to men of middle age: the building of new businesses, houses, marriages, alliances with women. Emergent wisdom interferes. Mellow phallos takes center stage, an aspect always present in masculinity but likely to have been dormant, overlooked, certainly undeveloped in younger, more callow males.

A suggestion of the feminine hangs about wisdom and age, yet it is not femininity. It is more gentle phallos, machismo softened by a realization that enough battles have been won, that it is time to gaze with wonder at one's grandchildren. Zest is present, but moderation qualifies everything; fatigue is found to be more accept-able. Tender wisdom was always a quality of phallos, however disregarded it may have been in athletic days. Phallos is excruciat-ingly sensitive, as the brocade curtain in the throne room of Jung's dream and the "naked flesh" suggest. Women can be amazed at the soft texture of the skin of a rock-hard erection, the cushioned head. Men know the delicateness of their testes and go to great pains to shield them from harm. Men are at their most vulnerable in the place which current jargon uses as an image of their courage ("he has balls"). Thus is the *coniunctio oppositorum* in wisdom presaged.

Jung's "ritual phallos," which he said he only understood decades after the dream, is the inner quality of masculinity, experienced in the behavior of the erection and translated psychologically into an archetypal masculine image. Jung's dream phallos upon its throne integrates the attributes of young, heroic, erectile vigor and old ruling wisdom, a uniting symbol for, in Elder's words, "a mysterious divine reality that cannot be apprehended otherwise."

Ritual is stereotyped action imaginally evoking a transpersonal or suprahistoric myth upon which the meaning of one's life depends. Ritual phallos points to the essential importance of the masculine as co-originating factor of creation. Ritual phallos is a statement of mythic fact, a means of celebrating maleness, a transmogrification of the male emblem of gender identification into inner symbol, showing forth masculine substance in image. For females, phallic ritual has been a way to acknowledge dependence upon phallos as the masculine agent of fruition and natal protection. Jung understood that pathological ritual, as in obsessive behavior, is a faulted personal striving for transpersonal meaning, made necessary by the absence of adequate collective ceremonies which connect inner meaning and outer experience.

Jung's early transpersonal phallic dream set the stage for his psychological explorations. The "single eye, gazing motionlessly upwards" portrays the staunchness of phallos, its focused atten-tion, its singularity of purpose, its relentless demand placed upon a male (and upon females as well, however differently). These strengths I needed in my early years at St. Clement's when my own phallic dream came upon me, before I had read of Jung's.

For all of his stated lifelong preoccupation with his childhood dream, Jung did not write much about phallos per se. He sub-sumed it in his investigation of the phallic gods of the Greeks,

Romans and Egyptians, and particularly Hermes-Mercurius, the psychopomp of the alchemical *opus*—which Jung called the medieval counterpart of psychoanalysis. As we shall see in chapter five, Jung found phallos at work mythologically in Mercurius, a god-image filled with spirit, *logos spermatikos,* the seminal word that enlivens psyche.[31]

The Power of the Mother

The issue of the mother is raised by Freud in his concern about castration and the "repudiation of the feminine," seen as the son's denial of the mother's claims for continuing containment of the son. It is also raised by Jung in his emphasis upon the journey of the hero, the aim of which is to escape and develop separately from the mother, who would keep her son safe within her psychic household. Each sees the mother as possessive, wanting her son at home for her benefit, not his, however much she may proclaim the opposite.

"Repudiation," in Freud's language, is the son's way of saying that he will not be possessed. The hero's journey, in Jung's language, is the son's way of saying that he will seek his fortune elsewhere than in his mother's embrace, however difficult the trials that engage him along his path. Both explanations clearly see the dangers of the mother for the son. No essential differentiation from the mother equals no masculinity, no phallos as a psychological possession of the son.

Writing in the mid-nineteenth century in his bachelor quarters in Basel, J. J. Bachofen put forth in his monumental *Das Mutterrecht* (in English, *Myth, Religion and the Mother Right*) the argument that an original matriarchate was present in the beginnings of psychohistory. This primal maternal domain "stands for the stage when ego consciousness is undeveloped and still embodied in nature and the world."[32] Bachofen builds this concept into a world-view, as in the following remarks:

> The mother is earlier than the son. The feminine has priority, while *masculine creativity only appears afterwards as a secondary phenomenon.* [Emphasis mine] Woman comes first, but man "becomes." . . . The female is primary, the male is only what comes out of her. . . . In a word, the woman first exists as a mother, and the man first exists as a son.

. . . Man becomes her plaything, the goat is her mount, the phallus her constant companion. . . . Everywhere the material, feminine, natural principle has the advantage.[33]

Such is Bachofen's concept of *das Mutterrecht,* lying beneath Freud's concern with the infant's relationship to his mother and Jung's archetypal understanding of the ego's dependence upon the collective unconscious as matrix.

Jung's hero, as emerging ego, must pull away from an originating feminine priority, establish itself as independent in its accomplishments, and then, as life nears its end, prepare to return whence it came. Both masculine independence and ego self-determination would seem to be transitory and illusory, since matrix, the mother principle, stands dominant at both birth and death. Its primacy prevails, whether or not it is visible, whether or not the process is understood by the son, whether or not he earns a certain heroic identification in the process of life. The game is rigged.

For Bachofen, even physical phallos, consisting as it does of *materia,* belongs to the mother principle. It is no wonder that Freud in his concern for the survival of the ego against the overwhelming power of instinct (nature, the mother, the id) tended to be pessimistic. "Nature," he wrote, "has her peculiarly effective mode of restricting us: she destroys us, coldly, cruelly, callously . . . it is the principal task of culture, its real *raison d'être,* to defend us against nature."[34] Jung was not pessimistic. He saw in the unconscious not only antagonism to the human process, but friendliness as well. For Jung, the unconscious was good mother as well as devouring mother. Nonetheless, it *was* mother.

In his recent book, *Jung's Struggle with Freud,* George Hogenson agrees that "Jung asserts the primacy of the mother in the structures of veneration. The father is nowhere to be seen." And again, "Jung's argument [is] that at the primordial level there is no father."[35] In both Freud and Jung, this is odd, given the importance they place in phallos. Since father effectively equals phallos, the placement of phallos in such a secondary, derivative position makes Freud's "bedrock" of penis envy and castration in psychoanalysis seem incongruous. Jung's hero's journey is similarly difficult to comprehend within his wider, archetypal understanding of the unconscious as matrix.

In both cases, the oddness can be understood if one realizes that both Freud and Jung lived in a culture wherein patriarchal supremacy was an unquestioned assumption. The compensation for this in these two men, so sensitive to the unconscious as a reality, was to elevate the mother to singular and primal importance. Then, in order to salvage masculinity from the compensation, as well as to establish it as an important partner with the primal maternal, culture for Freud and heroic ego consciousness for Jung were posited as counterparts.

To my mind, the process does not work. Masculinity, because it is inadequately based in psychoanalytic theory, becomes enemy of the unconscious for Freud and consort for Jung. The compensation, with correlative distortions, is unnecessary if a primal ground for archetypal phallos can be established in the psyche.

The mother is unquestionably important as a major factor in the development of masculine identity, perhaps even *the* major factor, since all males emerge from an experienced origin that is opposite in gender and in some ways inevitably oppositional in influence. The mother, however, is not masculine identity, nor does she stand, metaphysically, as the sole primal foundation of existence. Phallos is more than "the constant companion" of the mother, "her plaything" in Bachofen's terms. While Jung is undoubtedly correct in his understanding of the ego's dependence upon the unconscious, it cannot be simply assumed that ego equals masculinity (phallos) and that the unconscious equals mother. Origin is more than maternal, however invisible phallos might be in the passage of time after insemination.

James Hillman calls such a line of thinking—one that takes what is consciously apparent and conventional as true of the workings of the unconscious—a "naturalistic fallacy."[36] The problem with the naturalistic fallacy is that it impedes genuinely psychological thinking by taking literally analogies between the so-called natural world and the world of psyche. It is possible to argue a point psychologically, drawing from life experience and moving toward psychic similarity. I have done this with regard to phallos, using the characteristics of erection and male sexuality to establish the idea of inner archetypal phallos. Such logic, however, is not consistently valid. If a child has a less vital experience of father than of mother in early years, one cannot thereby necessarily argue that male participation in the origin is missing or essentially peripheral to the child's being. The child may not experience father as directly as mother, but archetypal phallos is present, whether or not masculine presence is outwardly experienced. Psychological thinking is paradoxical as well as linear. Hillman's notion calls attention to seemingly contradictory ideas, images and energies which actually fit 'together when viewed from a mythic standpoint. Hillman is authentically following and continuing Jung's conviction concerning the *coniunctio oppositorum* as a basic principle of psyche.

Mutterrecht, as a final solution to the question of masculine origin, participates in the naturalistic fallacy, as do psychoanalytic concepts that understand physical phallos as "nothing but" the possession of the cosmic and overarching mother, after the fashion of a boy's relationship to his female parent. An example of the complexity of using natural processes in support of psychological thinking is apparent in the use that might be made of the genetic studies of Money and Ehrhardt from Johns Hopkins University. They write:

> Nature's rule is, it would appear, that to masculinize, something must be added . . . suppressing the development of female characteristics. . . . In the case of anatomy, arrestment of development as a male is synonymous with development as a female . . . providing still further evidence that nature has more difficulty in differentiating the gender identity of the male than the female. Nature makes more errors in the male.[37]

This statement seems to substantiate Bachofen's claim of female primacy, and Freud's and Jung's acceptance of maternal dominance. It seems to contradict Hillman's notion of the naturalistic fallacy, since feminine nature reproduces itself and only with interference moves in a masculine direction. Moreover, Money and Ehrhardt call into question Freud's phallos-supporting castration theory, since females are not castrated males. Rather, males are further-developed females—the young clitoris becomes penis; labia tissue fuses and becomes scrotum. However, if penis envy is a psychological jealousy of greater masculine evolution, Freud's theory continues to hold and is given credence by the strenuous efforts of feminists to obtain equal social power with males.

Biologically, the "something" that must be added is androgen, the group of steroid hormones that develops masculine characteristics in the fetus. Androgen is contributed by a spermatazoon carrying the Y chromosome. Whence cometh the Y chromosome? Here one moves into the point of Hillman's warning about the naturalistic fallacy. What stands behind the mother, or beside her, at the origin of identity? The mother does not have a monopoly in the creation of life, regardless of her dominant presence in a child's earliest years, or in genetic formulations, or in psychoanalytic theory. A determining "something" is active but out of sight. To remain fixed within the naturalistic fallacy causes loss not only of psychological accuracy, it endorses loss of imaginal tone and timbre. Finally, it is a repetition, fancifully embroidered by the ego, of a limited and conventional viewpoint.

Both Freud and Jung assumed the importance of phallos psychologically without exploring the basis of the assumption. One can understand their interest in phallos when one grasps the importance of the mother in their thinking, and in subsequent psychoanalytic writing. Aside from the patriarchal culture already mentioned, there may be other reasons for the relative neglect of an element each considered to be crucial (recall that Jung said it preoccupied him all his life). References to phallos and derivative words and concepts in the *General Index to the Collected Works of C. G. Jung* take up hardly half a page of 735 pages, and most of these entries refer to phallic symbols used in the process of writing on something else. Jung's antipathy to what he deemed to be Freud's concretistic emphasis upon sexuality as the source of psychic energy was, of course, a factor, yet Jung's avoidance of focused attention upon male sexuality is hardly congruent with the importance he attached to the ritual phallos of his early dream.

Why did they not examine phallos more closely? My suspicion is that for Freud, a closer examination of the importance of penis and of castration would have led him into areas of investigation he wished to avoid, due to the rupture of his relationship with Jung. Jung's writing of *Symbols of Transformation* precipitated their break by making explicit the religio-mythic direction he was taking in opposition to his mentor. A deeper exploration of phallos might have taken Freud along the same path. Jung's reticence may have been a mirror image of Freud's. Even as Freud stopped short of paying deliberate attention to the collective unconscious, Jung resisted extending his research to physical sexuality, just as many Jungian analysts do to this day. Jung criticized the way in which Freud dealt with the dream Freud presented to Jung on board the ship that carried them to America in 1909. Freud, according to Jung, refused to give certain personal associations to the dream because, "I cannot risk my authority!"[38] Such a report by Jung might be understood as an unconscious self-confession of Jung's shadow projection upon Freud. But it may have been that Jung could afford to examine phallos only from the distance afforded him by his interest in symbolic referents.[39]

Whether or not Freud was leery of mystery and Jung was leery of physicality, the fact remains that neither did significant direct research work on phallos, and little has been done by their followers. This has resulted in a fundamental disservice to the importance of the archetypal masculine, a theoretical imbalance that cries out to be redressed.

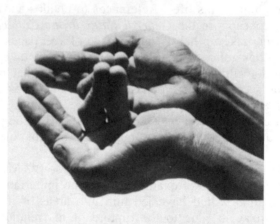

Indian hand gesture representing the *lingam* in the *yoni*.

4

On the Psychoid Nature of Phallos

At the still point of the turning world. Neither flesh nor fleshless;
Neither from nor towards; at the still point, there the dance is,
But neither arrest nor movement. And do not call it fixity,
Where past and future are gathered. Neither movement from nor
    towards,
Neither ascent nor decline. Except for the point, the still point,
There would be no dance, and there is only the dance.
I can only say, *there* we have been: but I cannot say where.
And I cannot say, how long, for that is to place it in time.
          —T. S. Eliot, "Burnt Norton," *Four Quartets*.

Neumann's Double—Phallos Concept

Erich Neumann (1905-1960) was a major interpreter of Jung and
a formidable scholar of psychomythology.[40] Neumann built an
impressive structure upon Bachofen's foundation of *das Mutterrecht,* the primacy and supremacy of the maternal in the psyche.
Psychoanalysis is indebted to Neumann for having provided an
evolutionary framework for Jung's research.

In *The Origins and History of Consciousness,* Neumann writes:

> Hippolytus himself is at the stage of critical resistance to the Great
> Mother, already conscious of himself as a young man struggling for
> autonomy and independence. This is evident from his repudiation of
> the Great Mother's advances and of her phallic, orgiastic sexuality.
> His "chastity," however, means far more than a rejection of sex; it
> signifies the coming to consciousness of the *"higher" masculinity*
> as opposed to the *"lower" phallic variety.* On the subjective level,
> it is the conscious realization of the *"solar" masculinity* which Bacho-
> fen contrasts with *"chthonic" masculinity.* This higher masculinity
> is correlated with light, the sun, the eye, and consciousness.[41] (Em-
> phasis mine)

Thus Neumann introduces his concept of the double phallos, so
to speak: the "lower" absorbed in the realm of sexuality, the domain
of the Great Mother, and the "higher" a development out and away
from this, in a spiritual direction. This is Epstein's sculpture of St.

Michael and the devil at Coventry, exactly. Lower phallos is caught in the underworld, the chthonic, unenlightened, vegetative and animal place, chained and enslaved to the orgiastic whims of the *magna mater*. Higher phallos turns its back on this fate, in Freud's words "repudiating" the Great Mother, and enters the realm of the solar masculine, where the eye can see, where sunlight abounds, where consciousness is free to expand. The formula becomes apparent: sexual phallos = servitude to the feminine = darkness; spiritual phallos = freedom from the feminine = light.

Later in *Origins,* Neumann restates the issue this way:

> Mythologically, the phallic-chthonic deities are companions of the Great Mother, not representatives of the specifically masculine. Psychologically, this means that phallic masculinity is still conditioned by the body and thus is under the rule of the Great Mother, whose instrument it remains.[42]

Here it is out in the open: a man interested in sexuality, the use of his body, his phallos, the physical agency of his masculinity, is ipso facto dominated by the mother, since all body, including phallos, is her instrument. All that is physical is mother. Instinctual phallos has no other source. According to Neumann, even males strongly evolved in a solar direction, "when they have the social leadership," may slip, "may still submit to the great chthonic fertility goddess and worship her in a feminine representative, because of the Great Mother's dominance in the masculine unconscious."[43]

Such a doctrine has bizzare implications: Use and enjoyment of body phallos beyond procreative necessity is seen as regressive and premasculine, essentially submissive, and rightly productive of guilt and inferiority. True masculine identity can be established only by denial of physical phallos—in a word, chastity. Only by translating physical phallos into symbol, as a means of escaping mother-ownership, can a male take his place in the company of adult men. Demeaning patriarchal attitudes toward women and toward men who display feminine characteristics, and the rape of nature for profit, are other implications of the viewpoint. One wonders how the symbolization of phallos can produce genuinely differentiated manhood. All phallic symbols, whether they be university towers, skyscrapers, church spires or interstellar rockets, are finally derivative of the mother, if phallos, itself, is her possession at the beginning. The reasoning is diabolically circular, permitting no escape. Men who

The double-phallos concept: *left,* carved wooden figure from Indonesia; *right,* statue of Christ in Chartres cathedral, with "higher" phallos (book, logos, the Word), in place of "lower" phallos.

have undertaken psychoanalytic treatment based upon these presuppositions have often met grief, and no wonder.

There is no doubt that a differentiation between chthonic and solar qualities of phallos can be made and is of value. The problem arises when one divorces them, as Neumann does—denigrating the chthonic as inherently feminine in character and thus inferior, while elevating the solar as evolved masculinity and superior, as if this were a natural law of the psyche. Both are forms of phallos; both can be good, both can be evil (an issue considered in chapter six). Each conditions the other.

The Basic Problem with Neumann

Neumann's treatment of the development of consciousness puts into focus the unconscious matrix of life, physically and psychologically, as well as the development of ego consciousness—which Neumann, following Jung, understands as a masculine-heroic phenomenon requiring separation from the mother, the *prima materia,* in order to emerge. There is, however, a serious flaw embedded in the double-phallos concept.

According to Neumann, the origin of the psyche and the human species is feminine, and only so. There is no functional or independent masculine presence in the beginning, no phallos. Neumann states that the maternal uroboros can be described as "living the cycle of its own life . . . the circular snake, the primal dragon of the beginning that bites its own tail, the *self-begetting* uroboros."[44] (Emphasis mine) One can find a suggestion of phallos in the image of the uroboros—the tail of the serpent entering its mouth—but it is no more than a hint, since the clear overall sense of the uroboric image is the "round," the most classic feminine form. In point of fact, Neumann does make mention of a "paternal uroboros" as a vague masculine presence in the beginning, actually as "the masculine spiritual aspect of the feminine."[45] This is but a weak suggestion of phallos, which remains an aspect of the feminine—the problem here addressed. The serious flaw is the absence of primal phallos as a coequal partner in Neumann's mythology of creation.

Neumann distinguishes four stages in masculine development, two passive and two active. The first is complete containment in the mother-belly or round, the uroboros. The second is matriarchal, with the male subservient to the mother-queen, separate from her,

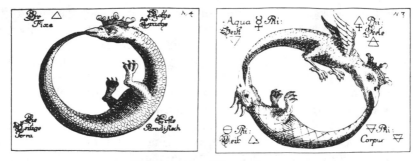

Two images of the uroboros.
(Eleazar, *Uraltes chymisches Werk,* 1760)

in a sense, but still tied to her service. The third, the first active stage, is that of the hero, a male's fight through trial and error to release himself from the mother and come into his own as a contributor to and possibly a ruler of the kingdom. The fourth is reproductive, where the male unites in intercourse with the mother-surrogate to produce a new generation of the species, a fulfillment of the primitive oedipal bond, but one step removed from it. Though active, the last two stages are nonetheless dependent upon a strong feminine presence. Never does the male stand as truly independent. Everything the hero does refers back to the Great Mother standing behind the process as ultimate. Neumann, following Freud and Jung, recapitulates Bachofen's *Mutterrecht,* and all of them in their foundational concepts recapitulate the Christian/Pauline diminishment of the body and sexuality.

There are two related problems with Neumann's view, both significant and troublesome. The first is a disparagement of the feminine in the characterization of phallos as inferior in its physical form and use. If the development of superior masculinity is equated with rejection of the physical (mother = matter = feminine), a particularly virulent form of patriarchy is implicitly encouraged. Neumann understood the spiritual qualities inherent in the evolution of "higher" phallos as human possibilities only within the context of masculine denial of the material and the feminine.

The other problem, particularly serious for Jungians, is the diminishment of the unconscious relative to the ego. The absence of primal phallos as co-originator of the human opus forces Neumann to posit an evolution which places "higher" phallos as the goal. The masculine heroic ego must emerge as victor; the chthonic unconscious must be conquered. Epstein may have portrayed the evils of the physical in masculine form, but according to Neumann the physical is always a disguise for the uroboric mother. The unconscious, therefore, becomes the base (and the baseness) upon which consciousness climbs to its height. Looked at from this perspective, Neumann seems strangely closer to Freud than to Jung. Neumann sees the id as the enemy of culture, and the chthonic unconscious as the enemy of solar phallos. Jung, in spite of the contradictions in his denoting of the unconscious as feminine, never countenanced ego consciousness, or solar phallos, as the goal of psychological activity. He recognized the autonomy and numinosity of the archetypal unconscious as primary to consciousness and worthy of committed attention and respect. Although Jung, to my knowledge, never openly criticized Neumann, he must have had second thoughts about the implications in his work. Neumann, in his tomes on consciousness and the Great Mother, moves inexorably in a conventional ego direction.

A problem can surface for a mature man in Jungian analysis. He is encouraged to move beyond his ego attainments and adaptation, his solar accomplishments, in the direction of the unconscious and the riches that there await him. The unconscious is a man's place of origin. In the evolution of an individual, it is essential to return to "the place" whence one came. As T. S. Eliot wrote, "And the end of all our exploring/ Will be to arrive where we started/ And know the place for the first time."[46] If a man's place is the realm of the mother—and thus, in a basic way, antagonistic—the connection will be impeded. If origin is understood only as feminine, male resistance is understandable, given the energy that has been expended in establishing masculinity as independent from the matrix. A man either remains where he is, bereft of the depths, or he gives in to the depths and surrenders what he has sought long to attain.

Phallos as god-image provides a solution to this quandry. Phallos as masculine source offers a man a way to return to the unconscious without surrendering his phallic identity. Phallic authority is not only reactive to the mother, as Neumann's double-phallos process suggests. Unless phallos is lodged independently in the depths of the unconscious, there is no masculine source to which a man can resort and depend upon as he moves beyond his ego attainments toward a return to his beginning . . . there is no masculine supporting structure in the source. The lack undercuts masculine return.

Phallos Protos **and the Psychoid Unconscious**

Jung in his later years investigated a dimension of the psyche which does much to rectify the absence of primal phallos in psychoanalytic theorizing. Jung came upon a concept that resolves knotty and paradoxical aspects of the problem of opposites, such as the one apparent in Neumann's thinking on the mythopsychological origin of the species.

I refer to what Jung called the psychoid unconscious. Aniela Jaffé, analyst and author, Jung's long-time student and his secretary in the last ten years of his life, says, "From 1946 onward, Jung described [the archetypes] as 'psychoid,' which means that they are not purely psychic but just as much physical in nature."[47]

Jung never systematically organized his writing on the psychoid unconscious and referred to it rarely, almost as though a reader who understood the general direction of his work would also understand this development in his thinking. Literally, psychoid means psyche-like. In calling something psychoid, one speaks of a psyche-like quality in that which is not ordinarily considered to be psyche, or psychological. It is a jarring term to use in connection with archetypes or the unconscious, since in common understanding both clearly reside within the realm of psyche. Using psychoid in reference to archetypes, Jung meant to denote the aspect of archetype that appeared in the physical world, its so-called outer manifestation. One can reverse the literal meaning of psychoid to get at what Jung meant. For example, psychoid applied to phallos indicates that the erect physical organ is a psyche-like instrument, that it is psyche as well as physis.

Jung wrote:

> The psychoid nature of the archetype contains very much more than can be included in a psychological explanation. It points to the sphere of the *unus mundus,* the unitary world, towards which the psychologist and the atomic physicist are converging along separate paths, producing independently . . . certain analogous auxiliary concepts. Although the *first step* in the cognitive process is to discriminate and divide, at the *second step* it will unite what has been divided, and an explanation will be satisfactory only when it achieves a synthesis.[48] (Emphasis mine)

Jung's writing of the "psychoid nature of the archetype" implies the psychoid unconscious, which he explicitly names elsewhere.[49]

The relationship between these two concepts, psychoid unconscious and *unus mundus,* is reciprocal, for each contains elements common to the other and both belong to the realm of the *coniunctio oppositorum,* the union of opposites, so essential to a grasp of Jung's thinking. The difference I am making in the use of the two is one of degree of evolution. I see the psychoid unconscious as a foundational concept, with the seed, the potential, of *unus mundus* within it. *Unus mundus* is goal. The idea I wish to convey at this point is the paradoxical nature they share, wherein psyche is "not purely psychic but just as much physical," as Jaffé stated.

One could hardly say that Jung discovered the unitary concept he named psychoid/*unus mundus;* mystics and other religious and poetic intuitives knew of its presence long before. Indeed, monotheism may be a collective cultural manifestation of the energy the notion has had in the psyche for millenia. Jung did, however, introduce the unitary concept into contemporary psychology at a time when physicists were moving in a similar direction. Einstein's famous equation, $E = mc^2$ (the total amount of energy, E, locked into a mass, m, is equal to that mass multiplied by the square of the velocity of light, c), indicates that "energy and matter are not the two faces of the universe, but simply two sides of the same face."[50] Jung's notion of an evolved unitary world, *unus mundus,* based upon the psychoid unconscious, has an importance to psychology similar to Einstein's theory of relativity in physics. It has been said that Einstein's equation points toward "untold riches . . . trapped in familiar substances that surround us—a new El Dorado, more fabulous than all the gold fields of the world, if only man could one day learn to release this energy and use it for his service."[51] The same may be said of the *unus mundus.*

The relativity between consciousness and the underground riches of the unconscious—and even more revolutionary, the complementary relationship between matter and nonmatter in the psychoid unconscious—presages a similar breakthrough in psychological awareness. One cannot perceive Einstein's relativity principle or Jung's psychoid unconscious with ordinary sensate left-brain capacities—here, again, one understands Hillman's warning against the naturalistic fallacy. Jung found that psyche and matter—energy and matter in Einstein's terms—were not essentially separate entities. One is the conversion of the other in the psychoid unconscious. At a point of synthesis, *unus mundus,* lies imaginal union: beyond "the first step," as Jung called it in the passage above, beyond the division into subject and object, spirit and matter, male and female, good and evil, all concepts which are necessary tools of conscious discrimination, there is a "second step"—the union of opposites.

The union manifests itself in the present in moments of ecstatic transcendence experienced by seers and sometimes by lovers. It serves as the basis of all religious systems that understand the world of ego consciousness as transitory. Knowledge of unity, and the experience of it, is the prized "second step" of synthesis and individuation.

Jung identified a quality in the psychoid unconscious,

> . . . an infringement to which I would give the name "transgressivity," because the archetypes are not found exclusively in the psychic sphere, but can occur just as much in circumstances that are not psychic (equivalence of an outward physical process with a psychic one).[52]

What is considered to be only physical can be just as well understood as psyche, and vice versa, seen from the psychoid perspective. Within the male body and psyche, for instance, an impetus to transform penis into phallos emanates from the deepest sources of instinct. According to Neumann, the deepest source of instinct is the realm of the maternal uroboros. But it is also the realm of the psychoid unconscious. Since the psychoid unconscious is characterized by archetypal transgressivity, physical phallos is simultaneously and paradoxically spiritual phallos; *"lower" phallos is also "higher" phallos*. Neumann's schema thus disappears. This understanding makes sense of Eliade's statement that sexuality, which perforce incorporates "lower" phallos, is the means of hierophany, conveying knowledge of the sacred. A man is not required to wrench himself from sexuality—to become chaste—in order to find what Neumann terms "higher" phallic masculinity. "Higher" and "lower" phallos are manifestations of a single psychoid reality.

Maternal uroboros is not the proprietress of instinct. Instinct, which includes sexuality, is phallic as well as wombic, so to speak, according to the principle of transgressivity. Just as chthonic phallos and solar phallos are mirror images of one another and infringe upon one another, so do the masculine and feminine elements collaborate in mythic sexual origin. Jung's psychoid concept intercepts Neumann's logic. The principle of transgressivity applied to origin means that psychic maternal origin is the obverse of paternal origin, however invisible phallos may be naturalistically. Here are "two sides of the same face" as in Einstein's energy-and-matter relativity principle. *Phallos protos* or patrix (Marion Woodman's term),[53] is as inevitable as is matrix.

Jung's *unus mundus* is the psychoid unconscious developed in a "postconscious" direction, closely paralleling what Jung called individuation. The unitary world and its transgressive quality are functional in the *unus mundus* as in the psychoid unconscious, but with a significant difference. In the psychoid unconscious, unitary and transgressive characteristics of the psyche exist in a condition of primitive nondifferentiation. *Unus mundus,* however, is a state of awareness where division and cohesion in the cognitive process are no longer understood only as streams of energy moving in opposite directions, as in Jung's "first step," but are complementary, moving along the same path. *Unus mundus,* as individuation, does not happen without great struggle and contention with life and the unconscious on an intentional basis. As with phallos, inner urge and purpose initiate and support the work.

Jung's psychology is both analytic ("first step") and synthetic ("second step") in principle. It strives to bring together differentiated opposites in a prospective unitary direction, suggestive of what might be called "new consciousness." New consciousness does not turn its back upon old things but brings them along into Jung's synthesis, the point beyond the struggle for differentiation. In *unus mundus,* chthonic phallos and solar phallos are as said in Zen:

Before enlightenment, chopping wood and hauling water;
After enlightenment, chopping wood and hauling water.

The Psychoid Aura

Jung wrote of "the psychoid aura that surrounds consciousness."[54] Aura is a distinctive air or quality characterizing a person or object. Aura is sometimes imaged, per se, but often sensed or intuited with the inner eye. In my early experience in the bed of my father, the aura was what I "saw" in his maleness—ritual phallos—beyond what I saw with my eyes—limp penis.

An aura indicates high value and importance; it is the conveyor of numinosity. In some cases, aura is actually seen with one's eyes as a faint glow around a person or an object. More often it is perceived by an inner sense. It conveys nuance, tone, and has a this-has-meaning-for-me quality about it. Aura indicates that by looking at one thing one perceives interiorly something more. Aura has a revelatory, crossover, from-one-dimension-to-another purpose. Consciousness, in Jung's statement, is enabled by aura to move beyond precise ego functioning into another sphere of psychic reality—one that has a psychoid quality.

Jung speaks of psychoid aura as though it were an everyday experience, which, of course, it is. For example, I have in my Pennsylvania kitchen a wide bay window that faces east, opening onto a large lawn surrounded by ranks of evergreen trees which screen out the road and neighboring houses. That window is a remarkable thing. It allows me to see the changes of season and the changes of the time of day. In the morning, the sun comes over the horizon of trees. In the evening, especially in the winter, when the sun descends behind the house, great shadows are cast from the house onto the lawn. The mixtures of blacks and greys against the white of the snow are preeminently suggestive. I sit at our round table within the enclave of the bay window, looking out at "the psychoid aura that surrounds consciousness." At one moment, I look into the foreboding darkness. I anticipate death. At another, I await the return of my wife from Scranton; at another, I know that without her, I might be catapulted from warmth to coldness, from inside the house to the hostile outside. Even with her return, I am not certain that the cold I look upon outside will not invade the house, making the outside, with its ominous loneliness, an in-the-house reality.

My experience is evidence to me of the psychoid aura surrounding consciousness. I know who I am as I look out that window; my day has been what it has been. The bills, upstairs, still need to be paid. Yet another reality imposes itself upon me as I sit there, watching the sun retire and the darkness sweep across my lawn. I see things with my eye, yet the inner eye sees more than my naked eye sees. I am touched by the unconscious, suggesting to my consciousness something other than what sensation gives to me. The lawn is still the lawn; the evergreens are what they are. They do not become something else, as in a drug-induced perception. What comes over me is mood; not mood as a disjuncture in thinking, but mood as an imaginal opening.

The capacity for transgressivity, for crossing-over, is at the heart of the psychoid unconscious as it is experienced by ordinary people. Jung called the human capacity to move imaginally from one level of reality to another the transcendent function.[55] My experience at the bay window is significant to me but not terribly unusual. To speak of the psychoid unconscious may sound abstruse, even esoteric, as though it were a factor beyond the capacity of the ordinary person to experience. It is not. Psychoid aura is an everyday perception, taking place in run-of-the-mill lives of people everywhere as they are touched by signals from the unconscious encouraging them to be still for a moment and to reflect upon that which comes.

The psychoid unconscious/*unus mundus* becomes the link one needs to move beyond the stasis and circularity resulting from Neumann's definition of physical phallos as derivative of the mother and contained within the archetypal feminine. In the psychoid beginning and within the *unus mundus* at the end of Jung's mythology of the psyche, there is no ultimate separation of flesh and spirit. Each transgresses into the other. Invisible spirit, as archetypally masculine, manifests itself in flesh; visible flesh, as archetypally feminine, manifests phallos. Phallos, *membrum virile,* is flesh *and* spirit—in a word, psychoid.

A Topographical Model of the Psyche, Inclusive of the Psychoid Unconscious

The chart opposite may assist the reader in grasping the place of the psychoid unconscious and *unus mundus* within the context of a larger whole. One can see how the basis for *unus mundus* is found in the primitive origins of the psychoid unconscious, before the differentiation of masculine and feminine. Once that differentiation has taken place, first matriarchy, then patriarchy, seizes power, resulting in "layers of consciousness," within which Neumann in his speculations about phallos found himself fixed. Neumann's double-phallos theory was a defense against what is here called Old Consciousness—the matriarchy, pressing from below. The double-phallos theory is in effect a justification of patriarchal superiority. Jung's concepts of the psychoid unconscious and *unus mundus* make such a justification unnecessary. New Consciousness, the movement beyond patriarchy, no longer requires the diminishment of the

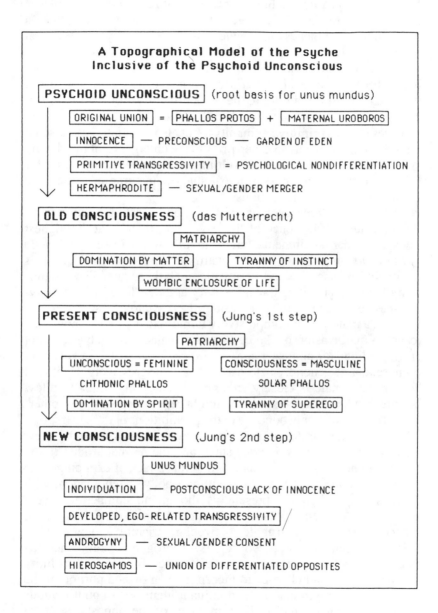

A Topographical Model of the Psyche
Inclusive of the Psychoid Unconscious

PSYCHOID UNCONSCIOUS (root basis for unus mundus)

ORIGINAL UNION = PHALLOS PROTOS + MATERNAL UROBOROS

INNOCENCE — PRECONSCIOUS — GARDEN OF EDEN

PRIMITIVE TRANSGRESSIVITY = PSYCHOLOGICAL NONDIFFERENTIATION

HERMAPHRODITE — SEXUAL/GENDER MERGER

OLD CONSCIOUSNESS (das Mutterrecht)

MATRIARCHY

DOMINATION BY MATTER   TYRANNY OF INSTINCT

WOMBIC ENCLOSURE OF LIFE

PRESENT CONSCIOUSNESS (Jung's 1st step)

PATRIARCHY

UNCONSCIOUS = FEMININE   CONSCIOUSNESS = MASCULINE

CHTHONIC PHALLOS   SOLAR PHALLOS

DOMINATION BY SPIRIT   TYRANNY OF SUPEREGO

NEW CONSCIOUSNESS (Jung's 2nd step)

UNUS MUNDUS

INDIVIDUATION — POSTCONSCIOUS LACK OF INNOCENCE

DEVELOPED, EGO-RELATED TRANSGRESSIVITY

ANDROGYNY — SEXUAL/GENDER CONSENT

HIEROSGAMOS — UNION OF DIFFERENTIATED OPPOSITES

feminine for phallic establishment. Masculinity finds its center as inner phallic reality. This, together with the anima, constitutes a restoration of wholeness in a male, made possible by the structural presence of *phallos protos* in the psychoid unconscious.

New Consciousness, however, is postconscious, in the sense that it is subservient to neither patriarchy nor matriarchy. It has passed through them. It is not prior to them, as is the psychoid unconscious. New Consciousness is aware of evil and of shadow as archetypal qualities (as was primitive humanity), but also, crucially, as personal qualities—an inconceivable step prior to the emergence of matriarchy and patriarchy. The conflict resulting from gender competition for primacy results in the possibility of shadow integration. When one is innocent, one is unconscious.

The marriage *(hierosgamos)* of matter and spirit in the *unus mundus* indicates the presence of the psychoid principle at the highest level of human attainment. Jung's great interest in the *coniunctio oppositorum* in alchemy points toward the same conclusion, as does his overall prospective and optimistic analytic stance. The dissimilarity between primitive transgressivity and developed transgressivity may be grasped by comparing the psychological difference between a male who is compulsively homosexual—for example, due to an anima invasion of the ego—and a male who is able to enact erotic feelings for another male by choice, whether he be generally homosexual or generally heterosexual. A transgressively developed heterosexual male is closely enough related to his anima to allow her the freedom of expression she might require, erotically or otherwise. He is no longer in bondage to the prohibitions of the superego.

A similar kind of difference exists between androgyny in the New Consciousness or *unus mundus* stage and the hermaphrodite in the psychoid unconscious. Hermaphroditism is a lack of explicit gender differentiation in nature, a "twin-within-a-body" phenomenon, with "organs" of both sexes present as though no competition were implicit or expected in gender separation. In that sense, it is blithe, innocent of the power struggles between matriarchy and patriarchy. It is preseparational and preconscious. Androgyny is altogether different. The androgyne knows the difference between masculinity and femininity, and chooses to incorporate an owned portion of the opposite gender into his or her dominant identity. An androgynous person does not pretend to be a member of the opposite sex. An androgynous male will not repress his feminine characteristics, how-

Alchemical image of hermaphrodite, sexually undifferentiated.
(*Rosarium philosophorum,* in *Artis auriferae,* 1593)

ever much he may, at times, decide to suppress them. He knows
that they are a part of him, he has worked on his ego resistance to
integrating them. He knows there will be times when he will choose
to think and perhaps behave according to the "her" within him. For
this reason Jung's concept of individuation, the acceptance and
living of one's personal myth, is a prefiguration of *unus mundus*.

One further word. I came to an appreciation of the psychoid/*unus
mundus* dimension of psyche through my appreciation for the mystery of the Eucharist in Christianity. In the Eucharist, common bread
and wine are taken, blessed, broken and given. The believing
receiver ingests not only the bread and wine but also the sacramental
body and blood of Christ, which I understand to be a symbol of the
Self. The Eucharist is a collective ritual of *unus mundus* based upon
the transgressive principle in the psychoid unconscious. Although
the Eucharistic service is highly stylized and overlaid with centuries
of ceremonial accretions, the "nub of the matter" is firmly imbedded
in its core. This is why respect for the rite remains for many persons,

myself included, when much of Christian tradition and practice have lost meaning. The Eucharist celebrates the paradoxical crossover inherent in the relationship between apparently incommensurable opposites—consciousness and the unconscious, for example, or matter and spirit—leading to the *coniunctio oppositorum*.

Axis Mundi As an Image of *Phallos Protos*

In the concept of the *axis mundi* I find an image that captures the importance of phallos as a primal image of masculinity, *phallos protos*. *Axis mundi* is not an easy image to work with, since Jung, at least in his published work, did not mention the term. Not so *anima mundi,* to which Jung gave great attention and importance.

> It is clear from a number of texts that the alchemists related their concept of the *anima mundi* on the one hand to the world soul in Plato's *Timaeus* and on the other to the Holy Spirit, who was present at the Creation and played the role of procreator, impregnating the waters with the seed of life, just as, later, he played a similar role in the *obumbratio* (overshadowing) of Mary.[56]

This passage is taken from Jung's long treatise on Mercurius, who was called, by one of Jung's alchemical sources, the *anima mundi* itself. There can be no doubt that the process Jung describes here, in its Holy Spirit aspect, is masculine. The choice of such words as procreator, impregnating, seed and "the overshadowing of Mary" so indicate. Later in the paragraph Jung comments that "here again matter and spirit are identical," a reflection of the psychoid quality of the Mercurial presence in the unconscious. The active words used in the quotation point to the involvement of phallos.

Jung used a feminine term, *anima mundi,* to describe masculine participation in creation, a situation which leads to the confusion in psychoanalytic thinking I have addressed in this work. One can understand how this happened. There seems to have been no masculine designation in alchemy symbolizing primal phallos as clearly as *anima mundi* represented primal soul. Anima is always feminine, as soul is. Something other than soul, however, is called for in the masculine energies required for creation. One comes to the need for *phallos protos,* which the alchemists found in the Holy Spirit. The confusion is compounded, however, by inclusion of a functionally masculine Holy Spirit within the *anima mundi*. The inclusion of

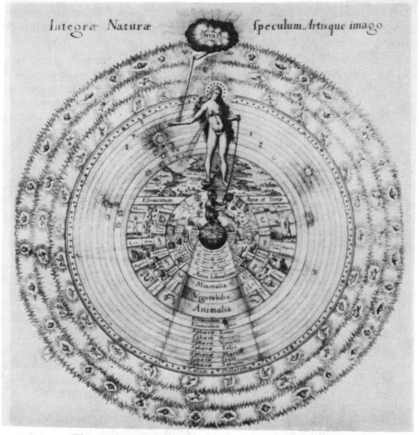

The *anima mundi* as world soul, guide of mankind.
(From Fludd, *Ultriusque cosmi,* 1617)

Mercurius helps the situation somewhat by his participation in both matter and spirit, but not enough, to my thinking. Both Holy Spirit and Mercurius are masculine images subservient to feminine soul.

The image of the *axis mundi* remedies this confusion. An axis is the central line on which something rotates or around which it is symmetrically arranged. The world axis is the primordial pivot around which the world turns. Since its shape is unquestionably phallic, and is of cosmic significance, it is an image that establishes primal masculine presence. It serves as a counterpart for Neumann's great round or maternal uroboros, and all circular or bowl-like symbols of the primal feminine. The axis of the world penetrates the great round of the earth, providing a means of connection with the cosmos.

Axis mundi is mentioned as an archetypal symbol rarely in psychoanalytic and image-oriented literature. I have not seen it specifically denoted as phallic. Roger Cook in *The Tree of Life* writes:

> The image of the Cosmic Tree or Tree of Life belongs to a coherent body of myths, rites, images and symbols which together make up what the historian of religion Mircea Eliade has called the "symbolism of the Centre." . . . This is particularly evident in man's obsession with the origins of things, with which all myths are ultimately concerned. The centre is, first and foremost, the point of "absolute beginning" where the latent energies of the sacred first broke through. . . . In the symbolic language of myth and religion it is often referred to as the "navel of the world," "Divine Egg," "Hidden Seed" or "Root of Roots"; and is also imagined as a vertical axis, the "cosmic axis" or "axis of the world" (Axis Mundi) which stands at the centre of the Universe and passes through the middle of the three cosmic zones, sky, earth and underworld. It is fixed at the heavenly end to either the Pole Star or the sun, the fixed points around which the heavenly bodies rotate. From here it descends through the disc of the earth into the world below.
>
> This idea of the cosmic axis . . . which is extremely ancient (fourth or third millenium BC) and widely diffused, is embodied primarily in three images, which are found in a great variety of forms throughout the world. These are the Pillar or Pole, the Tree and the Mountain.[57]

The combination of feminine and masculine images—navel and egg being feminine, seed and root masculine—points to the psychoid character of the symbol system referred to by Eliade and Cook. The specific presence of the axis, due to its phallic shape and penetrating function, is clearly the masculine aspect of the "Center" and the mythologem of origin. Since it is the core around which the natural world turns, *axis mundi* may contain within itself a suggestion of patriarchal claims for superiority. From the perspective of *unus mundus,* however, such a patriarchal claim is as nonsensical as that of sole matriarchal origin. Yet awareness of masculine participation in the mythologem of origin has no starting point without a primal symbolic presence able to stand on its own. New Consciousness will emerge in human beings only under circumstances of parity, never under reactive and derivative conditions. Such conditions

The *axis mundi* as World Tree.
(Detail of ceremonial cloth, Kroe, Sumatra)

always imply servitude and secondary status, which will produce psychological counterreactions and a battle for dominance, as was the case in Old Consciousness (matriarchal) and is in Present Consciousness (patriarchal).

Perhaps the most significant contributor to the understanding of *axis mundi* in modern scholarship is, again, Mircea Eliade in his work *Shamanism*. Since ancient times, shamans have been medicine men, most prevalent in Siberian and Indian tribes, who undergo rigorous training and initiation for a religious vocation of healing. Shamans engage *axis mundi* "by climbing it . . . undertak[ing] an ecstatic journey to the Center."[58] This is possible because the *axis mundi* as World Tree has its roots in the underworld, its trunk in the present, its foliage in heaven. On occasion, says Eliade, the tree may be inverted, with roots in the air, etc., additional evidence against the naturalistic fallacy.[59] At the point of shamanistic animal sacrifice, within the wigwam, the poles which support the structure and surround the smoke-hole—by means of which the shaman rises to the heavens with the offering—symbolize *axis mundi* and thus support a phallic interpretation. Eliade states, concerning this, that

> the axis, of course, passes through an opening, a "hole"; it is through this hole that the gods descend to earth and the dead to the subterranean regions; it is through the same hole that the soul of the shaman in ecstasy can fly up or down in the course of his celestial or infernal journeys.[60]

This is phallos, "flying" up and down through a "hole" in its search for out-of-ego ecstasy—the pleasure man seeks in erotic life, and a basic reason why Neumann's denigration of "lower phallos" is altogether inappropriate.

Axis mundi is the ancient image needed by men today as they experience the disintegration of patriarchal Present Consciousness. Surrender to reemerging matriarchy is not the solution, either cultural or personal. It is regressive and will produce, eventually, a stringent reemergent patriarchal attitude in vain defense of masculine identity. There is no need for males to fear females and act out such fear as tyrant or slave once a primary-process inner connection with phallos is engaged and dependably functional. *Axis mundi,* suggesting the rigorous, precarious heroism of the shaman, is just the ticket.

5

Archetypal Images of Phallos

Archetypal images are pictures of the way psyche functions. Generally speaking, the process of perceiving archetypal images is as follows: At the most basic level is the psychoid unconscious, primitive and undifferentiated energy, from which a "spark" evolves into pattern. Pattern presents itself to human beings as image—in old stories that have been handed down for generations, even eons, in dreams, and in current behavioral repetitions of typical patterns of human experience. With birth, pattern evolves as image, as in "mother," "father," "hunger," etc. If human life had no pattern, the history of the race would have to be recreated with each new birth. For this reason Jung suggested a kinship between archetype and instinct. Each infant comes into the world with a small but basic set of unlearned instincts. They are "given." So, also, is psychic patterning.

I have made a case for phallos as an essential factor coequal with the maternal in the fundamental psychoid unconscious. Phallos is an essential aspect of basic pattern. Basic pattern is the source-point of the sacred and numinous in human experience. Human experience is entwined at every moment with numinosity and meaning, communicated to communities and individuals through story and the implications of story in everyday human intercourse. Now I will turn to several old stories with archetypal images appearing as mythic figures who embody phallic patterning understood as god and hero.

Hermes

Hermes, the Greek god of commerce, invention, cunning, theft, also the messenger for the other gods of Olympus and the conductor of the dead to Hades, is an exemplar and image of phallos. Hermes' name was attached to piles of stones in ancient Greece used to demark boundaries and intersections of paths, roads and property lines. They were called herms. Rafael Lopez-Pedraza, in *Hermes and His Children,* says that these stone-heaps—herms—scattered across the countryside as were crucifixes in Europe in later days, were "archetypal image[s] of a God."[61] According to another source, herms were accumulated by "the custom of each passenger throwing a stone upon the daily increasing mass, in honor of the god."[62] Thus an erection, so to speak, was built up by the fraternity of men who passed by.

Fraternity is my emphasis. Men build up masculine and phallic identity by bonding with one another. Not all men are conscious of their bonding with other men or of how important it is for the establishment of masculine identity. Elder, quoted earlier, points out that while the original herm was a rather primitive stone-heap, in time it developed into a stone pillar topped by the head of Hermes and "featuring at its front an erect phallos with testicles . . . contrasting dramatically with the austere flat surface to which it is attached."[63] Such a development makes the phallic identity of the "heap of stones" all the more apparent.

Boundary marking is itself a phallic expression. An analysand returned from a visit to a modest cabin he and a male friend had built some years ago in a remote forest in the western United States. As he entered my office, he said, with tongue in cheek, "I have discovered the meaning of life." He had just gone to the cabin with a woman. The pride he felt in reconnecting with his property, and being there with the woman, was a "completion" experience. The cabin was in its original rustic condition. Over the years, he had been able to resist the many suggestions for improvements made by friends who had used it. This was of great satisfaction to him— a factor of his ownership. He had set up his psychological herm on that land and the fact that his herm had been respected, that he had the authority to demand respect, put him into immediate, experiential touch with his phallic identity. He and his ladyfriend greatly enjoyed the visit.

Hermes is not always acknowledged in such terms. Hermes stole Apollo's cattle as an infant, he moved among the gods as their messenger, he delivered the dead to Hades. Why, then, the outcropping of herms to denote boundaries?

It has to do with possession and ownership, an intrinsic characteristic of phallos. Phallic patterning predisposes a man to need to possess his place of entry. In a male, the possibility of losing phallos to, and in, a female reconstitutes the need for independence that a male knows from his encounter with the mother. Castration is the issue.

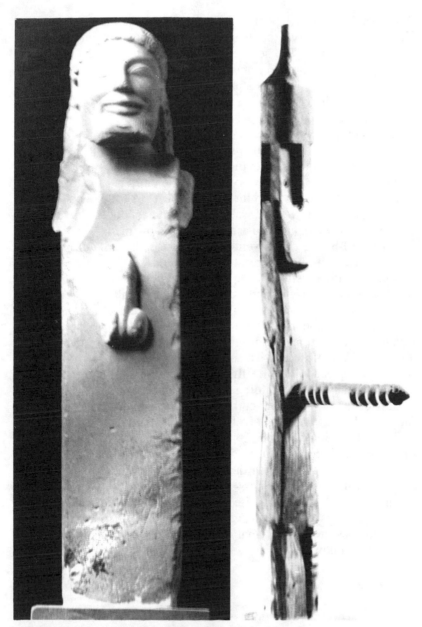

Left, marble pillar with head of Hermes, 6th cent. B.C. (National Museum, Athens); *right,* war god of the Zuni Indians of Mexico.

A male can be "swallowed up" by the female he enters (hence the *vagina dentata,* a vagina with teeth, ubiquitous symbol for the devouring mother). The sexual importance of possession is analogically extended to property and wealth of all kinds, since, in Jung's "first step," earth and earth's produce belong to the feminine realm. An antidote for castration on this level is ownership, a sense of substance which comes of possession.

Castration, however, is not the only issue. Male collegiality has its roots in respect for phallic presence among men, quite aside from feminine involvement. After the infant Hermes stole Apollo's cattle, he was caught by Apollo, who brought the child before great Zeus. Zeus ordered Hermes to return the cattle to Apollo, and Hermes obeyed. Inherent in this transaction was an acknowledgment of the authority of ownership. Zeus sat as judge in the matter, and Apollo, the standard-bearer of convention and conscious structuring, made his case. Hermes surrendered to the demands of the older gods. He accepted boundaries to his impetuosity. The acceptance of restrictions is included in Neumann's description of so-called higher phallic consciousness, restrictions which come with a male's realization that chthonic, impulsive, "take-it-all" phallic behavior at some point requires modification. Males realize this when they discover pleasure and feel secure as owners. The mutual recognition of the brotherhood of ownership leads to "the throwing of the stone upon the daily increasing mass," the building of the phallic herm.

This does not mean that chthonic phallic impulsivity is wrong or intrinsically "lower." Later in life, Hermes ushers the dead into the underworld, with which he is familiar. If one is not familiar with the chthonic underworld one cannot be a guide. Because Hermes knows chthonic phallos—as the thief who takes his brother's property, knowing no boundaries—he becomes herm, the figure representing respect for boundaries. Hermes exemplifies paradoxical psyche, as do psychoanalysts who must discover and deal with their own neuroses in personal analysis before they can become healers. One cannot know what one does not know.

Mercurius

Hermes and Mercury are images of the same pattern, Hermes Greek, Mercury Roman. Jung paid special attention to Mercurius, the alchemical form of Mercury, and attributed great importance to him.

Mercurius is not identical with Hermes, as no two mythic gods, even when they have the same name, are altogether alike. Differences among archetypal images are a reflection of how archetypal patterns vary in human behavior. The pattern has a similar structure so that it is recognizable from person to person, yet variations make each person unique. Archetypal images are like faces. Each face has eyes, a nose, a mouth, etc. as constant patterned components. At the same time, the composition of a face is individual.

Jung wrote that Mercurius "liv[es] in strange guises through the centuries, even into recent times."[64] As the spirit of the *opus* for medieval alchemists, Mercurius was referred to by Jung as

> the revealer of divine secrets, or in the form of gold . . . conceived to be the soul of the arcane substance . . . or the fructifier of the philosophical tree . . . the messenger of the gods, the hermeneut (interpreter) . . . the ithyphallic [erect] Hermes . . . the "continuous cohabitation" which is found in unalloyed form in the Tantric Shiva-Shakti concept.[65]

Thus, a paean of praise to the scoundrel Hermes-Mercurius, the thief, cunning from childhood, familiar with the chthonic underworld, strongly phallic.

Here is how Jung summarizes the multiple aspects of amazing Mercurius:

(1) Mercurius consists of all conceivable opposites. He is thus quite obviously a duality, but is named a unity in spite of the fact that his innumerable inner contradictions can dramatically fly apart into an equal number of disparate and apparently independent figures.
(2) He is both material and spiritual.
(3) He is the process by which the lower and material is transformed into the higher and spiritual, and vice versa.
(4) He is the devil, a redeeming psychopomp [guide into the unconscious], an evasive trickster, and God's reflection in physical nature.
(5) He is also the reflection of a mystical experience of the artifex that coincides with the *opus alchymicum*.
(6) As such, he represents on the one hand the self and on the other the individuation process and, because of the limitless number of his names, also the collective unconscious.[66]

In writing about Mercurius, Jung paid homage to his ritual phallos, the "subterranean God 'not to be named'" in the early dream that preoccupied him all his life. The summary above expresses in an extraordinary way the characteristics of psychoid phallos. But why phallos, the reader might ask. First, Mercurius is portrayed as male. He is understood to be male even in his dualistic aspect as male/female or when he appears as a female, as noted below. Second, Mercurius is quixotic—he comes and he goes, he rises and falls, as inexplicably as does phallos. Third, Mercurius disguises himself and hides, so that one is never quite sure where he is. He is a trickster, like phallos. He plays limp; he appears under the cover of foreskin; he hides between the legs and pretends he is not interested. Playing the gentleman, he lays the ground for seduction. Courting, he finds every kind of excuse to maneuvre his prey into a favorable situation. "May I buy you dinner?" "How about a drink?" "Would you like to go for a drive?" I have a daughter. I hear the telephone conversations with their veiled proposals. I also have a son. The telephone calls to him from girls are not the same. They inquire about how he is and what he's doing, they may even manipulate, but they do not often imitate phallos.

The spirit in Mercurius is male instinct, spirit corked up in the male body that wants expression through phallos. Uncorked, Mercurius "becomes the *one* animating principle of all created things," according to Jung.[67] The feminine awaits the animation of her potential, awaits ravishment, in Marion Woodman's terms.[68] The seed that leaps from phallos brings new life, her potential, into reality. Thus fathers protect young daughters, postponing fruition, and always will. Fathers know young men.

The spirit shows itself, or it does not. Enspirited phallos is the reason teenaged boys are embarrassed in public as individuals, even as in a group they are enlivened—as the boys discovering the Cerne Giant. Boys never know when phallos will appear. They are not sure of themselves as erectile beings; they are confident only when there is brotherhood to stand by them.

During the writing of this work, I spoke at the Analytical Psychology Club in New York. At the conclusion of the presentation, Erlo Van Waveren, an old and seasoned analyst who has since died, rose from his chair in the front row and exclaimed with fire, "Where is the spirit? You have read to us from your paper, but there can be no phallos without spirit! Spirit and phallos are the same!"

I was aghast at the public confrontation, but I knew, instantly, that he was correct. My presentation lacked vitality, a cardinal sin

Mercurius in the "philosopher's egg" (the alchemical vessel). He stands on the sun and the moon, symbols of his masculine/feminine nature. (*Mutus liber*, 1702)

against phallos. I laughed and agreed with him. The laughter broke the spell of a solar-logos masculinity in its superego form (often called the negative father complex). The animating spirit which transforms penis into phallos had been overwhelmed but was now breaking through.

Spirit comes to a man "bidden or unbidden," as Jung wrote on the lintel of his front door in Küsnacht.[69] Always it comes autonomously. Unbidden, it rises from the unconscious without warning, quickly making penis into phallos, boy into man, taking one by surprise. Bidden, it is prepared for, as in masculine initiation calculated to poultice spirit from the unconscious and make erections ready to inseminate. When it arrives, bidden or unbidden, phallos makes males feel alive, in awe of the transformation within themselves. They are fascinated by the appearance of power in what had been flaccid. In no wise does phallic spirit come from the mother *qua* mother, regardless of its manifestation in physical erection. It is profoundly and archetypally masculine.

The quixotic capability of Mercurius to appear and suddenly disappear, to be the agent by which the spirit is transformed into matter, identifies him with phallos. If the quicksilver factor is inhibited, as it was in me before my audience, a man becomes impotent; the Mercurial spirit is not present. Before that audience, I was caught by a fear of negative judgment in a sensitive area from senior analysts present whom I supposed were carriers of superior logos masculinity. This is exactly Freud's point about male-male castration. Neumann's dynamic worked. Primal, raw-spirited phallos was flattened. Fortunately, an opposite male dynamic shifted into place. My acknowledgment of the accuracy of Van Waveren's accusation, similar to Hermes before Zeus, my bonding with him by means of my laughter, containing a touch of the chthonic trickster, and the change that brotherhood initiated in my contact with the audience, all point to the rapid reappearance of Mercurius when phallic spirit moves out from under.

The spirit Mercurius, is, as Jung wrote, a guide. If he jumps up, one behaves in a certain way; if he disappears, desire is gone and it cannot be manufactured. Spirit activated means sexual interest constellated. Spirit deactivated means that the thrust is gone. Erection indicates the presence of Mercurius. Whether the context be the sexual bed or the delivery of a paper, the presence or absence of Mercurius is crucial. Externally, one might speak of "lower" phallos in bed and "higher" phallos at the podium, but beneath these distinctions Mercurius' presence or absence is the same issue, as Van Waveren pointed out. Mercurius' base is the psychoid unconscious, and from that point his energy flows, into chthonic *and* solar phallos, as archetypal patterns based upon common ground.

Mercurius as phallos is a way to understand what Jung meant when he called Mercurius "fructifier of the philosophical tree," quoted above. Fructify, in English, comes by way of French from a combination of the Latin *fructus,* fruit, and *facere,* to make. Mercurial phallos is the spirit-fructifier of the tree. It causes the tree to grow in the first place (erection), since an immature tree cannot bear fruit; then it makes the seed that flows from phallos, *logos spermatikos,* which in turn makes possible the fruit of the philosophical tree, knowledge. The tree can also be seen as maternal, which

phallos inseminates, and the fruit as the child of the inseminated mother. The tree Jung mentions, however, is the philosophical tree, more expressive of logos, the solar masculine principle. Jung's juxtaposition of fructifier and philosophical tree indicates the closeness of sexual and intellectual imagery as regards phallos. Chthonic phallos penetrates solar phallos. Chthonic phallos produces knowledge as the fruit of its semen-spirit. This is a good example of how Jung built upon Freud's sexual theories to investigate a process that continues to be instinctual in its imagery, but with much wider implications.[70]

The philosophical tree as phallos is seen above in a fourtcenth-century illustration from the Biblioteca Mediceo-Laurenziana in Florence.[71] It shows a dead, naked man lying on the ground with a great flowering tree rising from his groin. Piercing the man's chest is an arrow. Jung says it is the "arrow of Mercurius" and that the "*arbor philosophica* is growing out of him."[72]

Here we see the inextricable relationship between physical (chthonic) phallos and philosophical (solar) phallos, illustrated by the necessity of portraying one in terms of the other. The arrow of Mercurius may indicate the need one has to move away, for a time, from physical needs in order to accomplish logos tasks—a nod in the direction of Neumann. I do not refute such a shift in emphasis, when appropriate. It is the rejection of chthonic phallos in favor of solar that I challenge.

Dionysus

The god Dionysus is described by Walter Otto:

> Dionysus, himself, who raises life into the heights of ecstasy, is the suffering god. The raptures he brings rise from the innermost stirrings of that which lives. But wherever these depths are agitated, there, along with rapture and birth, rise up also horror and ruin.[73]

As seen from the perspective of Apollo, circumspect and careful, Dionysus is a strange god. Dionysus is slightly mad, impulsive, off-balance. Apollo is representative of Neumann's solar, "higher" phallos; his hallmark is not ecstasy, but order and regularity. Not so Dionysus. Dionysus' intrinsic connection with femininity causes him to emote with intensity, to feel rather than talk about feeling. Dionysian feeling is touched with hysteria. To an Apollonian, such excessiveness is unbearable. To a Dionysian, it belongs, even if it becomes tiresome to be always picking up the pieces. Neumann was obviously an Apollonian: Dionysian "lower" phallos must be transcended (read rejected).

Aeschylus called Dionysus "the womanly one"; Euripides, "the womanly stranger." At times he is called "man-womanish."[74] Dionysus' retinue of women circled about him in his erotic life and in his cult. His wife (Ariadne), his mother (Semele), his consort (Aphrodite) and his associates (Nymphs, Maenads) were his environment. His worshipers were the women of his rituals and festivals, who expressed themselves in wild excitement in the presence of ithyphallic representations carried in procession. A frenzy invaded

"The fusion and confusion of masculine and feminine . . . is expressed in the archetypal image of Dionysus." (Late Hellenistic stone carving; British Museum, London)

women in his ceremonies, even to the tearing up and devouring of their children. The males in his stories were Satyrs, Centaurs, Selini, all characteristic of lasciviousness. The proximity of women caught up in primitive abandon, rude male cohorts, and the drunken Silenus (the tutor of Dionysus) are suggestive of an underworld atmosphere characteristic of Dionysus—a quality of unimproved nature, stemming, as Walter Otto says, "from the primal depths of all that lives."[75] Thus are chthonic masculine (phallos) and chthonic feminine (womb), together expressing irrationality and orgy, bound together in the image of Dionysus.

And yet there is in *Larousse* the suggestion that Plato compared the old drunken Silenus, wobbling to and fro on his donkey, to Socrates, implying a wisdom in Dionysian bisexual phallos that is not at first apparent.[76] With all the wildness, one is tempted to dismiss Dionysus—his ecstatic women, his bare-bones phallic men, the drunkenness of his foolish tutor—as nonsense. Such judgment misses the point. Karl Kerényi, the mythologist, writes that

> the trickster god [such as Hermes or Dionysus] is the transpersonal source of a particular life-style and way of experiencing the world . . . transcend[ing] the scientific view of the world. . . . This aspect is utterly real and remains wihin the realm of natural experience. . . . Only at this point do we cross the boundary of experiences resting on sense impressions, but not the boundary of those which have undoubted psychic reality.[77]

The slightly mad qualities of Dionysus and his flock belong to psychic reality, and room must be made for them, whether or not Apollonians enjoy the coexistence. The fact that Dionysus contains within himself not only phallos but also strongly feminine aspects is cause for his suffering, referred to above by Otto. The fusion and confusion of masculine and feminine in the psychoid unconscious is expressed in the archetypal image of Dionysus.

Compared to straight-and-narrow Apollo, the Dionysian man feels unsure of himself. It is painful for a man to know that his maleness contains strong elements of femininity which seem to have no place in the collective canons of masculinity. He wants to belong but he can never quite manage it. Yet neither is he totally separate. The Dionysian male finds himself standing short of what he feels to be clear phallic identity. He does not have a sexual identity problem, as though he were pretending to be one gender while inwardly knowing himself to be the opposite. He knows himself to be male, and feels the male need that a woman can fulfill. Yet he shares with women in a way that no Apollonian can. He fears his admixture of the feminine excludes him from brotherhood. His suffering is communicated to the women who love him; they, as the Maenads, may go mad themselves with his lack of explicit definition.

Dionysus as archetypal image suggests several reasons why a psychologically hermaphroditic identity need not exclude a male from the company of men. First, there are more Dionysian males than the American Legion suspects, and many of them can be found drinking of the god's vine in bars where American businessmen, sportsmen, politicians and workmen, the apogee of contemporary Apollonian manhood, congregate. Second, women tend to like Dionysian men, as the festivals surrounding him indicate. Perhaps women now like Dionysian men more than ever, due to the influence of feminism, which in some women has raised a new-found respect for femininity. Men who attract women belong to the masculine brotherhood. Furthermore, the brotherhood itself changes as men come to know and respect their other side. Third, and most important, is the transgressivity that stands behind the Dionysian factor in the masculine personality. Solar masculinity, in patriarchy so compatible with ego, values straight-arrow, regularly defined, progressively linear phallos. The psychoid unconscious, however, objects, pressing for crossover, inclusion of the opposite.

The integration of chthonic phallos (with its overtones of the feminine) and solar phallos is the task of consciousness, a process inherent in the Dionysian image. To the extent that this takes place in a male, he moves closer to *unus mundus,* where fulfillment is the mirror image of suffering. The more Dionysus is accepted in a man's personality, the less crazy the image becomes.

Zeus and Ganymede

At the foot of the lake in Zurich, where the Bahnhofstrasse ends, there stands, at the most imposing place in the city, a fifteen-foot metal sculpture of Ganymede. When I arrived in Zurich in 1972, I

paid no attention to it. It was another modern sculpture, and Zurich is full of them. The Jung Institute, then, was fifteen blocks distant from the sculpture, along the lake and inland. One could easily walk from the lake-end of the Bahnhofstrasse to the Institute, which I did often: across the bridge over the Limmat, past the Opernhaus and the Kunsthaus. I can recall almost every shop, every turn in the route, now, as I write. Within a radius of some twenty blocks from that statue is the core of the city, ancient as well as modern. At the center of the core is the handsome statue of Ganymede.

If one does not know who Ganymede is, what difference does it make? He stands there, overlooking the crowds coming and going on the lake ferries—a youth of perhaps fifteen years, full of energy and life, lifting one arm skyward, the other touching down upon an eagle at his feet. He gazes at the eagle, as if it were his favorite dog.

A year after my arrival, I discovered the identity of Ganymede. He was Zeus's lover. According to *Larousse,*

> Zeus was charmed and, wishing to make him his favourite, had him swept up by an eagle . . . and brought to Olympus. It was also said that Zeus himself took the form of an eagle in order to carry off the fair adolescent.[78]

I was quite surprised. There, at the focal point of the most conventional city in the Western world was a boy about to be kidnapped by the highest god to become a sexual intimate and servant forever, the cupbearer of the gods, an adolescent who "rejoiced the eye of all by his beauty."[79]

Why? We know that Zeus was strongly attracted to females. His wives included Metis (Wisdom, whom he swallowed before she gave birth to Athene); Themis (Law, the mother of seasons and justice); Mnemosyne (mother of the Muses); Euronyme (mother of the Graces); and finally Hera, goddess of marriage and maternity, who was officially linked with his sovereignty. In the form of a bull, he violated Demeter, from which union Persephone was born. Beyond this, he pursued Titanesses, Nymphs, and even mortal women. Why Ganymede?

There may be a clue in *Larousse:* Zeus was "the supreme god who united in himself all the attributes of divinity."[80] All the attributes of divinity presumably include both masculine and feminine, involving characteristics of Hermes and Dionysus, both members of the Olympic family of gods. Zeus, in his femininity, may have been fascinated by the young and handsome Ganymede. Zeus, in his Hermetic aspect, may have given in to the impulse to steal that which belonged to Apollo. (This may explain the Apollonian Zurich fathers' placement of this sculpture at the center of their city: an unconscious need to deal with the shadow aspect of their circumspection.) Zeus, in his Dionysian aspect, may have felt a need occasionally to go wild, to connect with the suffering of the god who lives out his bisexual phallic nature.

On another level, Zeus's desire for Ganymede might be described as homosexual narcissism, a self-love which estranges a man from erotic connection with woman, requiring a partner who mirrors himself. Gods are known to preen, admire themselves, ask mortals for admiration, all narcissistic characteristics. Yet, aside from Zeus's interest in females, a small, hidden-away discovery in Jung's essay on "The Fish in Alchemy" suggests another possibility. In that essay, Jung quotes a statement by the medieval alchemist Arisleus that "the extremely small fish that dwells in the center of the universal sea . . . has the power to stop the largest ships."[81]

Ego, which thinks of itself as big and important, is less powerful than the invisible and seemingly inconsequential Self. Psyche is paradox. The Self, of course, is not inconsequential, no matter what the ego might think of it. In the case of Zeus and Ganymede, according to the working of psyche, Ganymede plays the small fish role, Zeus the largest ship. And, indeed, Ganymede stopped Zeus.

Jung again quotes Arisleus, and then another alchemist, Bernardus Trevisanus: "Nature is not improved save through its own nature." "Thus our material cannot be improved save through itself."[82]

The idea of the improvement of one's nature enters the picture. This puts an entirely different light on the issue of narcissism in the Zeus-Ganymede relationship. (One can argue whether it is possible for a god to improve himself, but that was dealt with in the "small-fish/large-ship" paradox.) Improvement might mean many things for Zeus. One could be the matter of age and youth. In spite of the promised glories of the approaching wise old man, men universally understand aging in terms of the diminishment of vigor and strength, and regret it. It is the loss of youthful chthonic phallos. Whether a man is homosexual or heterosexual, young men attract, however different the attraction. In homosexuality, the erotic attraction is irresistible. But whether a man be a grandfather fascinated with his grandson, or an aging gay looking for a younger version of himself, the archetypal dynamic of youth improving the experience of age holds. New phallos presents itself. As in homeopathic medicine, like cures like, *similia similibus curantur*. A man often needs a second man to help him in his integration of masculinity without prejudice to his erotic interest in females. This is a connection with phallos as source of life and libido, as masculine god-image, which— even—the archetypal image of a god might require.

D. H. Lawrence, in *Women in Love,* states the matter well:

> Gerald really loved Birkin, though he never quite believed in him. Birkin was too unreal; clever, whimsical, wonderful, but not practical enough. Gerald felt that his own understanding was much sounder and safer. Birkin was delightful, a wonderful spirit, but after all, not to be taken seriously, not quite to be counted on as a man among men. . . .
>
> Suddenly, he [Birkin] saw himself confronted with another problem—the problem of love and eternal conjunction between two men. Of course, this was necessary—it had been a necessity inside himself all his life—to love a man purely and fully. Of course, he had been loving Gerald all along, and all along denying it.[83]

At the end of the novel, Gerald walks into the mountains of Switzerland to die in a snow cave. Ursula, Birkin's wife, asks,

> "Did you need Gerald? Aren't I enough for you?"
>
> "No. You are enough for me as far as a woman is concerned. You are all women to me. But I wanted a man friend, as eternal as you and I are eternal . . . to make it complete, really happy, I wanted eternal union with a man, too, another kind of love."
>
> "You can't have two kinds of love . . . it's false, impossible."
>
> "I don't believe that," he answered.[84]

6

The Shadow Side of Phallos

Shadow of Chthonic Phallos

Jung's concept of the shadow is important to a work on phallos.
Jung coined this term to refer to aspects of the personality that have
predominantly negative characteristics—in his words, "the sum of
all those unpleasant qualities we like to hide, together with the
insufficiently developed functions and the contents of the personal
unconscious."[85] That definition is applicable to one's personal or
subjective unconscious, since shadow traits ordinarily are repressed,
hidden, forgotten or never fully developed. But Jung also wrote of
shadow as an archetypal component of the psyche, "the dangerous
aspect of the unrecognized dark half of the personality."[86] Archetypal
shadow is what we perceive as evil, understood as principle rather
than as personal attribute.

Neumann's double-phallos concept by definition places chthonic
phallos in the shadow. Epstein's sculpture of St. Michael and the
devil portrays this attitude. The placement of chthonic phallos, per
se, in shadow is a serious distortion of psychological reality, as I
have demonstrated. It is a sign of domination by a solar patriarchal
attitude. Definitions of masculinity that equate chthonic phallos with
masculine shadow are not tenable.

Still, chthonic phallos unquestionably has a dark aspect—partly
caused by its rejection as a valuable participant in developing consciousness, and partly inherent, as darkness and threat always are
present in archetypal patterns. However difficult it may be to integrate
the shadow into ego consciousness, Jung's basic point is a simple
one: there can be no light without shadow. Both chthonic and solar
phallos make sense as concepts only when their antithesis is included
in one's understanding. The mistake is made when chthonic phallos
is seen as nothing but the shadow of solar phallos, rather than its
antithesis. The accurate way to understand chthonic phallos is to see
it in the same way one understands solar phallos, as containing both
good and evil factors. Chthonic phallos is both ego-alien and ego-syntonic. Were it not both, physical phallos could not be the instrument
for hierophany that Eliade sees it to be.

93

The shadow of chthonic phallos can be characterized by its gross-ness, brutality and carelessness. It can be characterized by its insa-tiable desire and possessiveness, by its unmitigated power needs, by a kind of mad drivenness, by the mayhem of war and ruthless competition it occasions. Life is replete with examples of its stupid and devastating behavior, the "man-eater," as Jung's mother called it in his childhood dream.

One particularly virulent example was the subject of a magazine article entitled, "The End of the Ride." It told of Lawrence Singleton, a fifty-one-year-old man, and Mary Vincent, a fifteen-year-old whom Singleton picked up as a hitchhiker en route from the Bay area to Los Angeles on September 29, 1978. Before their first day was over, Singleton picked up two men in his van, and the three together drugged, raped and sodomized Vincent. Late that night, she was left to die in a coastal canyon, naked, dazed, with both her arms chopped off at the elbow. Mary Vincent survived that night; Singleton is in prison.

It is startling to read what Singleton said about himself in an interview for the magazine. He claimed that Mary Vincent was a prostitute, that she gained possession of a knife in the glove compart-ment of his van, that she was prepared to emasculate him if he did not take her where she wanted to go. He is quoted: "Everything I did was for survival. . . . This crime could not have been committed without her help."[87] Singleton justified his conquest of Vincent as self-preservation. He may, indeed, have seen it to be so. If Singleton suffered from a particularly malevolent devouring mother complex, he could have experienced Vincent—or anyone else—as a deadly enemy and thus acted to demolish the menace. Phallos is obviously capable of such horror, particularly when the threat of castration—real or imagined—enters the picture from either a feminine or a masculine source. Phallos is a primitive jealous god who will tolerate no serious challenge to his authority. Rare is the man who has never felt the urge to destroy whomever or whatever threatened the center of his identity.

To understand shadow phallos in connection with male impulse for self-protection does not justify Singleton's behavior. Much that resides in the shadow depths belongs there rather than in outward behavior. Neither anything Mary Vincent did on that day nor any inner psychic dynamic of Singleton's vindicates his violence toward Vincent. Unquestionably Singleton's psychic state was dominated by darkness. There is more to darkness, however, than such shadow behavior. Underworld is dark, chthonic phallos is dark, but not all of underworld is shadow. Chthonic phallos is the means by which a man moves through ego limitation to ecstatic merger with the archetypal world in sexuality. It is the numinous source of his being as a male. It is the silent god within, prompting his creative action, standing behind his erectile strength, facilitating the explosion of his fertilizing seed. Chthonic phallos is the hidden source of masculine power, dark because of hiddenness, capable of catastrophic rage, but capable also of tender love and keen attention, based upon instinctual nature and need. What happens in darkness to a male tells the story of his contact with divinity, whether that divinity be light or shadow, or a mixture of both. Darkness is chthonic. Darkness itself is not evil. Darkness is the home of the spark.

The poet Robert Bly catches the positive importance of chthonic phallos in an article entitled "What Men Really Want." Bly says,

> When I look out at my audiences, perhaps half the young males are what I'd call soft. They're lovely, valuable people—I like them—and they're not interested in harming the earth, or starting wars, or working for corporations. There's something favorable toward life in their whole general mood and style of living. But something's wrong. There's not much energy in them. They are life-preserving but not exactly life-giving.[88]

Bly tells of leading a conference of forty young men in New Mexico for ten days:

> Often the younger males would begin to talk and within five minutes they would be weeping. The amount of grief and anguish in the younger males was astounding! The river was deep. . . . They had learned to be receptive, and it wasn't enough to carry their marriages. In every relationship something fierce is needed once in a while; both the man and the woman need to have it.[89]

Bly goes on to discuss Grimm's fairy tale "Iron John" ("Iron Hans" in the original). Something strange is happening in the forest near the king's castle. People are disappearing. One day a hunter goes with his dog to investigate. They come across a pond. A hand reaches up from the pond, grabs the dog and pulls it down. The hunter returns to the village for help; a team of men go to drain the pond. At the bottom is a very large man covered with reddish hair the color of rusted iron. The men capture him and take him to the castle's village, where the king orders him to be placed in a cage in the square. One day, the king's young son is playing near the cage. His golden ball rolls into the cage, and the wild man seizes it. He will return it to the prince if the prince will release him from the cage. To do so, the prince must fetch the key which the wild man knows is under the queen's pillow. The king and queen are away, so the prince snatches the key and opens the cage. When Iron John walks out, the prince is terrified that his mother will be angry. So the wild man scoops him up, places him on his shoulders, and off they go into the forest, where the prince will learn the secrets of manhood.[90]

This is not the complete fairy tale, but it is all that Bly uses to make his point. Iron John is chthonic phallos—wild, rough, fierce—precisely what is missing in Bly's soft young men. From the viewpoint of the queen, chthonic phallos is unsuited for civilized living, to be kept locked away and out of reach to her precious son. From the prince's standpoint, however, contact with Iron John is an essential part of his masculine wholeness—the golden ball that rolls into the wild man's cage. Untamed chthonic phallos imprisoned within mother-domesticity is Freud's feared feminization in the male. At the same time, Freud saw the id as implacably hostile to consciousness. Freud was more aware of the importance of physical penis/phallos than was Neumann, but he never resolved this contradiction. To do so, as already suggested, would have required a movement in Jung's direction, understanding archetype and instinct as dual manifestations of the same psychic energy.

The issue of chthonic phallos is important to men who have a strong spiritual component in their lives and/or a dominant solar masculinity. What do they do with the sweaty, hairy, animal phallos represented by Iron John? It is not only the mother's desire to keep her son close and compatible with her style of life that damages chthonic phallos. The father participates, as the king did in the fairy tale. The father who has lost the power and raw energy of chthonic phallos would also deny it to the son. In practical terms, this may become manifest in the abrogation of the father's masculine authority, which by default goes to the mother. And often when the father experiences the return of phallic energy, he leaves the domestic scene to act it out. In such cases, the son is left to fend for himself in a maternal—and often hostile—environment, with no male role-model.

The danger for the son is in his unconscious adoption of the value structure of the mother, with her antagonistic attitude (often unconscious) toward Iron John. Either the son inches closer to Freud's feminization or he becomes prematurely solar in his life goals, adapting himself to a masculine stance devoid of sexuality—or both. His spirituality becomes brittle and technical without the hot breath of chthonic phallos, half-there, rational and without inspiration. This is the dogmatism against which Rudolf Otto wrote as he investigated the *numinosum*. Fascination and wonder are gone, since both are inextricably related to the rise and fall, death and resurrection, of chthonic phallos.

The fundamental resolution to the problem of the shadow is its integration by the ego. The integration of the shadow aspects of a man's personality means that the shadow is not denied, however alien it may be to his persona-image or his sense of ego propriety. Shadow creeps through a crack in the ego's armor. It shows in despised dream images which must be taken as a portrayal of the dreamer's shadow personality. Often the body tells, and this is especially important in sexual matters. Penis may refuse to rise or remain risen; sperm may refuse to come. Even more important, in shadow-related situations, are occasions when Iron John erupts in full force, bringing on a possession which a man cannot and does not really want to control. I have an analysand who worries that he loses himself in sexual situations, that his careful and loving phallic quality disappears and he becomes a sexual machine, oblivious to the subjective reality of his partner. He considers loss of ego control to be dangerous. Yet on these occasions he comes close to the hierophany of which Eliade writes—he is in touch with the numinous in himself. (Every man is "in touch" with chthonic phallos in the most cursory masturbation.) My analysand is experiencing the raw power of chthonic phallos.

My analysand is surprised by his partner's positive reaction to this transformation in himself; often she herself is archetypally seized—her chthonic *yin* welcomes his chthonic *yang*. Raw phallos can produce this readiness, and more, in a partner, even when, as shadow, sometimes it overwhelms and destroys. Desire for ecstasy, shared by males everywhere, proves the error of Neumann's diminishment of chthonic phallos, as nothing else does. Males always search for it.

Still, the issue of shadow hangs on, particularly when rape, stupid drivenness and atrocity—the Singleton syndrome—come into view. Integration of the shadow side is essential if anything like the full power of chthonic phallos is to be allowed into a man's life. A man must take chances with raw sexuality, testing its boundaries. Otherwise he will hide from it, judge it severely, dance around it, be plagued with guilt and try all manner of things to convert it to solar phallic consciousness, thus losing his chthonic entry into the divine. Such a man runs the serious risk of becoming a shell of masculinity, with the key to experiencing his fullness hidden under the queen's pillow—with the cooperation of the king, or "ruling dominant of collective consciousness," as Jungians love to say.

Integration of the shadow side of chthonic phallos for a male means accepting the rapist in himself, with all the ugliness and brutality that implies. A man must be aware that chthonic phallos can lead to both rapture and murder. He cannot be genuinely aware of the closeness of the two without the integration of shadow: an intellectual and existential awareness of evil in every area of his life, including sexuality as hierophany. Hierophany, after all, can be a manifestation of evil in the divine.

No "good" factor in the human psyche is under all circumstances good; no "evil" factor is in all circumstances evil. One might justifiably criticize a man for being wild and uncivilized, yet wildness and uncivilized behaviour by chthonic phallos move male consciousness toward a realization of the sacred in the depths. Civilized phallic behaviour never realizes this destiny, however prized its gentlemanliness. It only hints at it. The young prince must go into the forest to live for a time with Iron John. A gentleman must know that he is also a beast and know the appropriate times to become that beast—that is the integration of shadow chthonic phallos. The prince must of course emerge from the forest, but with his eyes open to the duality of his nature.

The analysand mentioned above is a spiritual seeker who for years has been confused by his extraordinary zest and ability in love making, as though one contradicted the other. He feels inwardly obligated to make a choice—rampant sexuality or spiritual progress. It is not chthonic phallos itself that makes him leery of sex, but rather the implications of shadow attached to

The rapist, shadow side of chthonic phallos.
(*Abduction of the Sabine Women,* by Jan Mueller, 16th cent. engraving)

it—power, gratification, lust, the loss of ego boundaries in the flowering of ecstasy.

Conventional Christian teaching has the similar effect of separating sensual pleasure from spirituality. While this man is not a particularly keen Christian, he was raised in the church and he lives in a culture permeated by the implications of the sexual-spiritual opposition. His problem is not much alleviated by his Jungian reading, which often seems to substantiate the need for a choice. The way for him would seem to be personal acceptance of the inevitability of certain shadow elements in his chthonic sexuality, together with an understanding of how these elements might indeed bring him closer than he realized to his spiritual goals.

One can find examples of Christian spirituality that actually use images of the ravishing shadow chthonic phallos to describe God's active pursuit of humanity. In Anglican John Donne's seventeenth-century "Holy Sonnet XIV," the human soul is understood as feminine relative to the phallic deity, whose quarry she is. The shadowlike images are emphasized by me:

> *Batter* my heart, three-personed God, for you
> As yet but knock, breathe, shine, and seek to mend.
> That I may rise and stand, *o'erthrow me and bend*
> *Your force to break, blow, burn* and make me new.
> I, like an usurped town to another due,
> Labor to admit you, but oh, to no end!
> Reason, your viceroy in me, me should defend,
> But is captived, and proves weak or untrue.
> Yet dearly I love you and would be loved fain,
> But am betrothed unto your enemy.
> *Divorce me,* untie, or *break that knot* again,
> *Take me to you, imprison me,* for I,
> Except you *enthrall me,* shall never be free,
> Nor ever chaste except you *ravish me.*[91]

To ravish is to so impress oneself upon another that the other is overcome and torn apart, with transformation implicit in the action.[92] A potentially new creature emerges from the dark-night attack, one who is no longer innocent or bonded to childhood expectations and maternal nurture and comfort: the polite knock, the gentle breathing, the reassuring morning light, the soothing, the simple mend. The inbreaking of chthonic phallos, including shadow aspects, is required for transformation and rebirth. Pounding, breaking, forcing, taking are actions of phallos obedient to its nature. The paradox of ravishment as the means of chasteness explains Jung's insistence upon the need for shadow integration. One cannot be pure without knowing impurity as one's own experience; one can find only naive enlightenment without the discovery of evil within oneself.

The desire for an inbreaking of the divine is not masochistic unless one understands all ego-threatening experience as inherently and finally destructive. No religiously sensitive person would do so. Masochism is taking pleasure in suffering, not submitting oneself to a necessary suffering for the sake of psychological growth and development. In this sense, the refusal of suffering is more closely related to neurotic ego defense, to stalemate, to anxiety. Psychologically understood, anxiety is artificial suffering, visited upon oneself compulsively, not the willingness to undergo terrors that are necessary for either birth or rebirth. In such a way can humanity, relative to the phallic divinity, be understood as archetypally feminine—awaiting, requiring, an intercourse that leads to new creation.

Shadow of Solar Phallos

One might not think of solar phallos as having a shadow dimension, so commonly is chthonic phallos made to carry the shadow of masculine enlightenment. *The New York Times* recently carried the story of a male college president in Massachusetts, highly regarded by his peers and his community. He was indicted on charges of sexual assault against two male students and of paying the family of one of the students $10,000 for keeping the incident confidential.[93]

Whatever the legal outcome, the college president's career is ruined, perhaps his life as well. Blame for the ruin is almost surely to be placed at the feet of chthonic phallos with its insatiable appetite and its nefarious disregard for limitation. Neumann's "lower" phallos is commonly understood as the ugly shadow underside of a man such as this—"universally praised," regarded as "a fine man" his board of directors "trusted," respected educator, rescuing the college he headed in a time of crisis, church organist, family man with five children, two of them adopted, and on and on. This man has sterling solar masculine qualities.

It is important to understand that the college president's story is not an example of the shadow of solar phallos. It is chthonic phallos gone bad, perhaps due to the tendency solar phallos has to denigrate chthonic phallos. In this story it can be seen how dangerous that tendency can be. Because a man is "upstanding" (ironically, a solar phallic designation) he may be intolerant of chthonic phallos, following the dictates of patriarchy. Chthonic phallos becomes functional shadow of solar phallos, even when, psychologically, it is not.

What, then, is the shadow of solar phallos?

Solar, from the Latin for sun, represents enlightenment, the result, as Neumann would have it, of a strenuous masculine effort to pull oneself up from the dank and primordial miseries of maternal nature. In ordinary life, this translates into the pride a man takes in his social reputation, his ability to stand tall in public review, the attainments he would like noted in his obituary, the important things he talks about at cocktail parties (before the alcohol regresses him into chthonic fantasy). Solar phallos is the political party a man belongs to, the papers he reads, the alumni associations he supports, the legal agreements he signs, or, even more basically, his word being as good as his bond. Solar phallos is a man's profession, the adequacy of his financial and moral support of his woman and his offspring. Solar phallos is the way a man takes care of his house, the attention he pays to his worth, the way he tinkers with and polishes his car. Solar phallos is the attainment goals he has for his children, particularly his male children. It is how a man speaks, what he speaks about, how he follows words with action.

Solar phallos is in fact word, *logos* ("word" in Greek), which in Jung's thinking is the substance of masculinity. For Jung, logos is to masculinity as eros is to femininity. Where logos thinks and transforms thinking into word, and understands this as accomplishment, eros feels and transforms feeling into relatedness, and understands that as accomplishment. For solar masculinity, nothing is of decided value unless it can be *established*. Establishment is in the patriarchal view the victory of solar phallos over chthonic phallos—one reason for the commonly held notion that chthonic phallos is the shadow of solar phallos.

Solar men love institutionalization; it is their narcissism, a reflection of their standing in the world. Show a man an institution, give him authority over it, and he sees his legitimacy confirmed. Women and their attraction, even his own children, are decoration when a man is in thrall to institution, his proof that he is whole even when he is not.

The shadow aspect of solar phallos is the pollution of the fatherly task. A father will work diligently to rear a child as a credit to him, and simultaneously tyrannize the child so that he or she can hardly think or feel anything but what the father has planned. By setting the boundaries of possibility, the father determines, ex cathedra, what is true and what is false, what the child can and cannot do for a living, who the child can and cannot marry. In one case that I know, a patriarch attempted to dictate even what the adult daughter of a friend could eat. He loudly demanded, at a public event, "Joanne, what's the matter with you? What do you mean you don't eat meat? Are you crazy or what?" The friend's daughter, an independent woman well into her fifties, was speechless at the affront, as is often the case when one meets the shadow of the solar masculine.

The unconscious purpose of solar phallic shadow is to disenfranchise, to castrate the obstreperous and misbehaving inferior—male or female—much as the witch-mother does. Both understand themselves to be royal in their domains, and both behave in a similar manner. (In a female, the damage done to her animus is as devastating as the more concrete damage done to a male's sense of phallic power.) I remember walking into the office of a senior priest in New York whose parish gave substantial financial support to St. Clement's in its early and most vulnerable years. The cardinal rector was seated with a male friend, chatting. As I rounded the corner of his room, he greeted me with a great smile, "How are you, boy?" Had I been willing to risk the money his parish gave my mission I would have replied, "Just fine, mother-fucker." My rage was enormous. I can feel it today, twenty years later. I knew then, with little psychoanalytic knowledge, that he meant to demean, to imply that I was his "nigger." Now I call this male-male castration. Then I needed neither Freud nor Jung to know that I had been insulted.

The patronizing attitude is a clear indication of shadow solar phallos. The patron is in the driver's seat, having earned his credentials by submitting to the same offensive behavior he now imposes upon his inferior object. Rather than make the younger or weaker person more comfortable, he transfers his own past humiliations on to the other, exactly what Jung meant by projection. If the vulnerable person takes the insult, he or she is rewarded. Family therapists call this dynamic a negative interactional system, which they treat through direct confrontation within a gathered family. Effective as intervention is within a family, what is one to do with a supervisor or even a president of the United States who functions in the way of solar phallic shadow? Alas, the archetypes act in just such an inflated manner, as do myriads of persons enacting archetypal solar masculine patterns in every byway of human interaction.

Solar phallos knows itself to be correct, and has proved it by its institutional accomplishments. It is therefore correlated with light, having risen above the horizon of darkness, the realm of the unconscious. In the light, one is not lost in the shadows of ignorance; one is ready to bite the bullet of hardship for the sake of honor. A solar man wants the facts. Factuality, and the technical effectuality that comes from empiricism, gives solar masculine consciousness the illusion of strength and solidarity that seems impregnable, standing on the base of rational order. Sentiment is not to interfere. Feminine relatedness must take a back seat on the bus. Relatedness is all right for neighborhood parties, weddings with the proper people, Christmas cards, dignified home decoration, and even, in some cases, with brotherhood groups, such as taking a sauna at a health club after a heady night out.

The solar patron wants the power of direction, an archetypal phallic attitude. Shadow phallos, both chthonic and solar, is motivated by conquest, whether the object be body or mind. Where shadow chthonic phallos would overcome by physical force, shadow solar phallos seeks to subdue whatever spirit or intelligence is susceptible to its thrust, in the interest of "truth." What appears to be patronal generosity has a number of secret strings attached which bind the recipient to the benefactor and hinder independence. The ingratitude of others is the lament of solar phallic shadow. The grand plan has not worked; the object of largesse is wrong and must be punished. Many a husband and father, having made great sacrifices as patron of his wife and children, turns against them when he feels they disobey his direction and dishonor his leadership. How dare they! It becomes obvious that his interest was in attaining a position of power in his personal or professional life in order to control those dependent upon him. He feels his obligation, his right, to rule. It is not the individuals in his family or firm that are primary. It is power, vested in his authority and institutional allegiance.

Shadow solar phallos is the brutal underside of Apollonian

"Men who resist serious reflection on the pomposity and inflation of patriarchal assumptions of supremacy are priapic psychologically."
—page 106. (Priapus weighing himself; House of the Vettii, Pompeii, 1st cent. A.D.)

order and correctness. Logos domination can lead to a degree of destruction only hinted at by shadow chthonic phallos behavior. The highest potential of masculine solar consciousness—spirituality, intellectual and institutional leadership—can tyrannize whatever is considered to be in error, whoever cannot "measure up" (an oblique reference to the interest males have in phallic size). The tyranny is all the more devastating due to the cultural admiration of solar masculine attributes, behind which the shadow qualities fester. A classic example of collective solar phallic shadow was the American Civil War of 1861–1865, when hundreds of thousands of young men were slaughtered in the bucolic countryside of a new nation in defense of the principles of union on the one hand and states' rights on the other. Ideological principles are indigenous to solar masculinity. They have the ring of truth about them, but the underside, the shadow, of righteousness and purity is organized mayhem and death.

Solar patriarchal superiority is currently under attack. Feminism, the peace movement, gay rights, environmentalism, civil liberties, even animal rights, all, in their own way, threaten the dominance of the great phallic sun god. It is wasteful for men to defend their phallic power in an undifferentiated manner, as though all criticism of patriarchal accomplishment were a threat of literal castration, to be warded off at all costs. As Jung long ago pointed out, to be one-sided psychologically exposes one to serious mental and/or physical illness—or worse, contaminating others with the illness one avoids in oneself. For men to shirk the negative aspect of phallos, whether chthonic or solar, demonstrates ignorance and cowardice, not the wisdom and courage that eventually come with shadow integration. Admitting weakness paradoxically brings strength.

A modicum of humility does not destroy the effectiveness of phallos. A most bizarre and pitiful figure is that of Priapus, the Roman god whose enormous erection will not go away. Men who resist serious reflection on the pomposity and inflation of patriarchal assumptions of supremacy are priapic psychologically. Their vaunted psychological erections, never relaxed, make them a laughing stock. On a global scale, the amusement has become deadly black comedy. The nations are constructing nuclear phallos after nuclear phallos, aiming them at one another, playing boys' games of challenge—comparing whose emission might shoot the farthest. Such is the mortal danger of the shadow of self-righteous solar masculinity.

One final word on masculine differentiation and the anima. Jung wrote that behind the shadow in a man's unconscious stands the figure of the anima, his feminine contrasexual soul image, and behind the anima stands the archetypal figure of the wise old man, an image of authentic solar masculine refinement. To reach maturation, in a Jungian sense, it is necessary for a man first to work through his shadow—the negative/evil aspects of chthonic and solar phallos. He then must deal with his inner femininity and its requirements for relatedness. Hidden behind these two enormous psychological tasks is the possibility of wisdom, the knowledge and stature that come only with age and long self-reflection.

Wisdom in a man will not appear without these two primary confrontations with the unconscious, both of which are major challenges to his ego solidity. The difficulties involved in what Jung called *auseinandersetzung*—"having-it-out" with the shadow and the anima—cannot be overstated. Often a man feels as though this night sea journey will be the end of him, that his ego, his personality as he knows it, will not survive. One of the greatest terrors is the loneliness of the conflict; hardly anyone can help, sometimes not even an analyst. The specter of evil and femininity as personal attributes can undo the strongest man. In the midst of chaos it can appear preferable to attempt to stand pat in the shambles of one's life, uprighteously phallic, undaunted. Jung calls this "the regressive restoration of the persona," essentially a retreat, a lethal error.[94] Without a blow to inflated phallic pride, no wisdom is possible. One continues to build bombs, the bigger the better.

7

Phallos Out of the Ordinary

Two Dreams of Men

For a Jungian psychoanalyst, it is impossible to deal with psyche without including dreams, which come to human beings daily, albeit under cover of darkness. Darkness suggests another world, making dreams invaluable sources of life information obscured during waking hours when the ego with its defenses is more fully in command. Analytic work cannot be done without them, for they provide a "third voice" mediating between the analyst and the analysand, correcting both.

Dreams are reworkings of the residue of the dreamer's present life; they are also visitations into the present of the oldest of the old, the archetypes and psychoid unconscious. They are important to any modern person who seeks to take the whole of life seriously. The correlation of old and new within the structure and story of a dream is a way in which the transgressive quality of the psychoid unconscious becomes known to ordinary human beings.

The two dreams I present here are not as clearly archetypal or as expressive of the psychoid unconscious as Jung's dream or mine, told earlier. The dreams in this chapter have more interstitial, related-to-the-life-of-the-dreamer material within them. Phallic god-images are present, however, under the surface, and it is with these that I deal. Connections with a dreamer's personal life facilitate a crossover in personal awareness, a grasping of the presence of the archetypal in what otherwise might be experienced as banal daily routine. In analytic treatment, dreams undergo a more thorough investigation than is appropriate here, where I deliberately limit myself to a consideration of phallic presence.

Dream one

Kind of a strange mixture of hero worship, my favorite instrument and transsexual identities.
　It begins with my meeting in an old house belonging to Bee-

thoven, who is acting like a young, boyish brat. He looks twenty-one, overweight, with frazzled hair and very impudent. My vision of him comes from my experience of the Mozart persona in *Amadeus,* both play and movie. But the peculiar thing is, I can swear that this character was played by a young woman the last time I saw him. He's my hero, since I once wrote a whole screenplay about Beethoven, but he's boyish, long-haired, and used to be a woman! Next I am at a piano and playing some manuscript pages from a man who sits nearby. This composer is a contemporary . . . like a typical Westsider, thirtyish, dark haired and handsome. But he is too pushy and bitchy about how I should play his music. Well, the notes are not really all there or they're not readable. So he's really an asshole badgering me about his music.

There's a pause. Then I'm at a table, again looking over some music. And this man (the composer) comes up and tosses his *cock* onto the table in front of me; it's not only the shaft and balls, but the *root* of the cock, as if a small tree-stump is there! I'm surprised, of course, since this means he must be a transsexual (like the Beethoven character) and in fact, he simply has a hole, or vagina, where his cock used to be.

The central image of the dream is the removable male genitalia of the bitchy composer, whose music cannot be played because it is not all there. The genitalia are thrown upon the table in contempt. The dream, overall, has a distinct Dionysian flavor—masculinity permeated by a just-under-the-surface femininity—which the dreamer acknowledges in his opening comment about transsexual identities. The trickster is present in full force, tossing his cock, balls and root on the table in defiance. The masculine organs are like a Groucho Marx nose that can be taken off at will and used against an adversary. It is the trickster to a "t," with his maddening capacity to play with his sexuality.

Here is an appearance of Mercurius in his role of trickster, actually moving into the dream life of a contemporary man as a constituent part of that man's unconscious personality. Mercurius the composer is described in the dream in terms that sound like someone else describing the dreamer. The dreamer is thus mirroring the god. The god appears to the dreamer in disguise, as an image of the dreamer's personal myth.

The trickster appears here as "the typical Westsider"—for whom the dreamer has an association suggesting trickster. "The typical Westsider" is not an objective definition of trickster. In

Scranton, the trickster might be "the typical Southsider," in another city, "the typical Eastender." The point is that the trickster tricks, and whomever the dreamer understands as tricky is the image that trickster uses to make his presence known.

The reason the trickster tricks is that the ego thinks itself to be much too smart. The ego is actually quite stupid. Because of its derivation from the Self, the ego presumes to take on the characteristics of the Self and count them as its own. (Ego psychologists can get quite off-base on this issue, encouraging the ego to take all that it can get, for the sake of what is called a good "ego-image.") The unconscious objects; it tells the story as it really is. "You think you have a solid connection with your masculinity, solid enough to pass judgment on others—pushy, bitchy, impudent? Look at this! Look how easily your cock and balls come off! Look at the hole underneath your superior attitude."

The trickster is the unconscious judging the judgments of the ego. The trickster pokes holes through the ego's inflation. In the cock image, trickster tells the dreamer to include irrationality in himself, not simply play with it inconsequentially. The dreamer has in fact a Dionysian air about him, which he eschews in the interests of social propriety. As a man properly brought up and schooled, he indulges in antics covertly, as a joke, a defiance of convention. On one occasion, he made love with his girlfriend on a fire-escape thirty stories above the street, in a building he entered on a whim. The escapade was Dionysian, but does not indicate the intentional inclusion of the god in his life. Similar episodes in the dreamer's life suggest that he acts out in a superficial way what solar phallos disapproves of. The impulsiveness denies him a genuine experience of the suffering of Dionysus. The god's torturous inner masculine-feminine struggle is avoided. The dream calls attention to the dreamer's refusal to seriously own his Dionysian qualities by attributing them to the young Beethoven or the other bitchy composer.

As we saw in our brief look at Dionysus, there is a wisdom in masculine-feminine coexistence in a male. It is not a wisdom easily accepted by one schooled in logos solar masculinity, since it finds little affirmation in patriarchal role modeling. Trickster's humiliating confrontation, exposing the dreamer's underground Dionysian side, his inner secret, suggests the need to seriously acknowledge his own myth, regardless of outer expectations. That is the path of individuation. Here is a way that Mercurius as dream actor is a messenger of and to the gods. Mercurius tells the dreamer that he belongs to Dionysus and, as it were, tells Dionysus that the dreamer is a potentially conscious follower of the god as an inner daemon.

When Jungians talk about a god appearing in a dream, they are referring to a manifestation such as the one just discussed. Mercurius or Dionysus does not necessarily appear as one might expect, any more than Christ need appear in dreams literally as Jesus himself. The god's presence is known by the pattern of the dream; one must know the pattern to be able to see his image, hidden, say, behind the guise of a bitchy composer. The unconscous is not hindered by modern man's having lost connection with a folk wisdom that communicated a knowledge of pattern to our ancestors. It nods to our ego reality in the mise en scène, the setting, and the *dramatis personae*. There the dreamer's associations are essential, as in "the typical Westsider." It is of course difficult for a modern dreamer, without assistance, to recognize Dionysus in his associations. But one can see how important the identification of this phallic god can be to a dreamer's self-awareness. The task, one way or the other, is for the ego to get the message.

Dream two

There is a huge, estatelike church. A Mass is going to be said on the grounds outside. Gene is going to be the priest. There is an altar on the lawn and a lot of benches. I take a bench in back. The whole tone of the Mass is liberal and I think that this is because it is an Anglican Mass.

We start with a long hymn. It is difficult for me to sing, so I mouth the words. Gene leaves the altar and walks around the benches and goes off. Soon he returns as the hymn ends.

Some people come by and I have to make room. I realize I am wearing a hat. I think people will think I am Jewish. I take it off as it is inappropriate to wear a hat at Mass.

The scene changes. I am inside the house. I am inside a room with four or five people. They seem older. I feel the need to masturbate as I am under great sexual tension. I try to get away but I feel it is too risky. I end up looking through drawers to choose clothing.

My focus here is on the "great sexual tension" that has come upon the dreamer during the preparation for the Mass, which I, as priest, am to celebrate. A connection is made in the dreamer's unconscious between his analysis and the ritual of the Mass. The dreamer is a Roman Catholic well schooled in the teachings of his church. He continues to practice his religion, especially at times of crisis in his life. I am an Anglican.

Jung wrote extensively on the Mass as a ritual of psychological transformation.[95] The awareness of sexual tension is the first signal a man receives of the proximity of phallos, anticipating the transformation of flaccid penis into erect member. The god is on the horizon. That this awareness is coincident with a celebration of the Mass might seem strange unless one realizes that the Mass is a means of connecting with the transgressive dynamic in the psychoid unconscious. In a collective mode of expression—the Mass, expressing the mysterious union of opposites in the *unus mundus*—autonomous stirrings of phallos are felt. Phallos begins to awake from his dormancy even as the tantric Kundalini serpent arises from sleep, coiled around an inner *lingam*.[96]

Tantric religious practices center around an experience of the relationship between sexuality and the divine.[97] Tantrikas come together as lovers, intimately connecting their bodies short of intercourse, and then stop, for there, on the threshold of union, a door opens to the greatest of mysteries. The sacred reveals itself. The tantrikas then withdraw from sexual activity to admire, to worship, to enter a sacred space which the sexual energy between the partners has made manifest. Tantra is a highly disciplined physical-spiritual religious exercise and cannot be entered into without knowledge and preparation. Yet every lover knows something of the truth of the tantric discovery. Lovers, however, are unprepared to make demands upon themselves, to withdraw, meditate upon and worship that which their pleasure opens to them, as do tantrikas. They have no preparation for entering into the cosmic event brought on by their erotic drives. In the West, the church blesses marriages, but seems to have little awareness of the mystery it presumes to consecrate.

This dreamer has the potential to understand such things, as the dream points out by the introduction of phallic stirrings in the midst of the Mass. He has yet to make the conscious connection between sexuality and the holy that the dream suggests. That is why the dream came to him.

What about the dreamer's "need to masturbate?" Men often feel guilt about masturbating because of the stigma of self-indulgence attached to it. Yet masturbation is normal and ubiquitous—and according to the testimony of many women, sexual intercourse is a permitted masturbation for men more often than men realize. Masturbation can be understood as a man's acknowledgment and enjoyment of phallos, for its and his own sake.

In the above dream, the urge to masturbate comes upon the dreamer in the context of a liberal Mass. In the Mass, one worships God sacramentally incarnate in the mystery of consecrated bread and wine. In masturbation, unseen phallos becomes palpable phallos and is likewise owned and confessed. The god is enjoyed, even as the Presbyterian *Shorter Catechism* instructs one to "glorify God and enjoy Him forever."[98] In the Mass, ritual actions accompany transformation. The same is true in masturbation. The act is secret, however, not collective as is the Mass. Psychoanalysts are more aware than others of the rich ritual environment men construct for masturbation, both concretely and in fantasy. Phallic worship today, as a man's personal and tangible homage to his inner life force, takes the form of masturbation. It is therefore appropriate that the dreamer's "need to masturbate" occurs within the context of the Mass. Both the Mass, as a ritual containing psychic energy moving from the exterior to the interior, and the need for masturbation, containing psychic energy moving from the interior to the exterior, coalesce in a transpersonal, sacred ground. Here again is found the union of opposites, the hallmark of the psychoid unconscious, presaging *unus mundus*.

The appearance of phallos in male sexuality is connected with pleasure and the promise of instinctual fulfillment. A common language is used in sexuality and religion to describe the state attained. Noteworthy are rapture, ecstasy, bliss. Masturbation rarely does more than suggest such a level of fulfillment. Only sexual engagement with a partner, when the boundaries of ego are transcended in a merger with the other, produces an experience of raw archetypal presence—rapture, ecstasy, bliss. Neither is such an occurrence likely to happen at Mass, so structured and ego-syntonic are such collective ceremonies. Religious rapture tends to descend upon one in solitude, ordinarily the condition of masturbation. Masturbation in the dream, then, points to a personal connection with the god, one that is celebrated collectively in the Mass. Masturbation and the Mass are related inversely. What takes place in both masturbation and Mass is recollection and promise, a remembrance of things past, or anamnesis, and an intimation of possibility, or hope. Since instinct and archetype are inextricably related, it should come as no surprise that both suggest their presence in religion and sexuality, as in this dream. Creation and re-creation are the motifs that link each with the other.

Homosexuality

Is homosexuality pathological?

Any sexuality, or no sexuality at all, can be pathological. The case of the college president (in chapter six) is ample demonstration of this. But homosexuality per se? The question presents itself in a consideration of phallos because of the great homosexual attraction to phallos and the fear in so-called straight men that any interest in phallos indicates latent homosexuality. Historian John Boswell of Yale University has stated that the collective problem with being gay is that most homosexuals are not "inferior insiders," as are women, or "outsiders," as are blacks, but are people with no category whatsoever in social history. Homosexuals are not perceived as members of a subgroup within the community but as people similar to everyone else but with depraved sexual interests.[99] Such an analysis accounts for the fear men have of what Vanggaard calls the homosexual radical within themselves (discussed in chapter two).[100] Homosexuality implies nonexistence on a collective basis, the denial of both ego and Self.

Boswell has dealt with the historical reasons for this exclusion in his monumental book, *Christianity, Social Tolerance and Homosexuality*. My interest here is in the fascination phallos has for men who are closely related to their homosexual radical. Is the phallically oriented sexuality of such men depraved, pathological and criminal, as stated in the recent U.S. Supreme Court decision upholding the Georgia law against sodomy?[101]

Image of sodomy as insemination of masculine spirit.
(From Vitruvius, *De architectura*, 1511)

Were phallos only an instrument of service to the Great Mother—derivative of her and returning to her in obedience to her magnetic attraction as source—a case might be made for homosexuality as an aberration of basic instinctual energy. The goal of homosexual phallos is penetration, as is all phallos, but not the penetration of a female. It could be said that penetration of a female by a homosexual man is an embellishment of the obvious, since a feminine quality is already strongly present in his ego. This is the ordinary way of looking at homosexuality: an abundance of the feminine in the male ego, forcing libido in a male direction as a compensation. One seeks in sexual desire that which is missing from the ego. In the homosexual, the powerful Great Mother in the unconscious has invaded the ego, permeating it, feminizing it, homosexualizing it. Consequently, it is commonly believed that male homosexuals have problems with unstable ego formation and boundaries and that with ego-strengthening therapy heterosexuality will emerge. Femininity will be eased out of the ego and into the unconscious, where it belongs. Patriarchy, conditioned by solar phallos, will take its place.

It must be said that there is a certain truth in such an evaluation. The experienced analyst can discern when homosexuality is simply an aberrance, a consequence of an overfeminized ego, and work toward its masculinization. It is to be noticed, however, that even the most rigorous psychoanalytic treatment rarely excises phallos from the erotic interest of men with an active homosexual radical. If the psychological situation were a matter only of maternal distancing and the analysand's resolve to take up the cudgels of heroic stance, the "cure" ratio would be much greater than it is. The point is that men, be they homosexual, bisexual or heterosexual, have an archetypal connection with phallos that cannot—indeed, should not—be cured, since it is not an illness. How a man deals with his sexuality is where pathology enters the picture—a question involving collective expectations and judgments and their effect upon the subject, as Boswell suggests. Sexuality, in itself, including the omnipresent homosexual radical in men, is not, and never has been, pathological. Were this not so, Epstein's portrayal of Michael-spirit triumphant over devil-sensuality would be accurate.

It is as wrong for psychoanalysts to judge where a man should be on the continuum of the homosexual radical as it would be for them to judge his masculinity by the size of his penis. Cultural norms, comparisons, statistical studies, gradations in size as well as placement on scales are naturalistic fallacies. The psychoanalytic issue is the presence of phallos in the psychic life of a man, what the god demands and what the response of ego will be to the demands—the process of individuation. Involved in this process is a working-through of whatever in the outer situation causes a man to feel pathological because of his psychological connection with phallos. In this way, a new attitude toward both inner and outer demand is born, aided by knowledge of *phallos protos* in the unconscious.

The power of *phallos protos* in the male psyche is a sign of the god's determination to claim a man as his own. This is a religious understanding. God places his finger upon a person and demands a personal response. Both the Jewish and Christian scriptures are replete with examples of initiative on the part of God. The choice of the prophet Isaiah, the voice proclaiming Jesus as the son of God at his baptism, the falling of the scales from Paul's eyes on the Damascus road are familiar examples. The dynamic of sacred pursuit is itself phallic in nature, whether the aggressive god be clothed in accepted Western religious image or felt directly by a man as the urging of instinctual phallos. The latter is an immediate experience of the *numen;* the former is mediated by tradition. The whole of humanity, the potential church, is understood to be the bride of Christ by St. Paul, underlining the phallic quality in divine initiative.[102] Ganymede, the youth abducted by Zeus, was the name given to homosexuals in medieval times, expressing phallos as god-image pursuing a chosen man.[103] That homosexuals consider themselves somehow special, a breed apart, thus seems to be something more than a brash compensation for their status difficulties.

An article in *The New York Times* reported on the 1985 convention of the American Psychological Association in Los Angeles.[104] The APA in 1973 had reclassified homosexuality from "mental illness" to "psychological disorder." There continues to be unease with even that milder designation. At the 1985 convention a panel discussion took place entitled, "Parental Support of Gay Children: Empirical, Experimental and Organizational Perspectives." The parents rejected "the widely held belief that domineering mothers and absent fathers are the reasons a child becomes homosexual. . . . In talking with thousands of families, the panelists said, no consistent psychological pattern had emerged in the parents of homosexuals."

A spokesperson for the parents said, "We have learned that there is no choice. No one chooses to be gay. We believe that our gay children are born that way, that homosexuality, like heterosexuality, is innate." It might be said that such an observation is patently self-serving. Certainly it oversimplifies the issue. Nevertheless, the statement is worth consideration from the perspective of archetypal phallic initiative, for the parents' claim points to a source and director of libido other than the vicissitudes of childhood experience. Jung's conviction that the unconscious has a dynamism independent of ego experience and intention—that it functions as "an autonomous mode of cognition," as Eliade wrote, that it is the source of Otto's *numinosum* and *mysterium tremendum*—points to a similar kind of awareness. Innateness must not be understood only biologically. Conceptually, innateness is a bridging concept linking instinct, which is biological, and archetype, which is psychological. The transgressive or crossover characteristic of the psychoid unconscious indicates that biological and psychological heredity are "two sides of one face."

In explaining Jung's idea of the collective unconscious and its archetypal patterning I commonly use a home-grown metaphor of a ship, representing the individual ego, crossing the ocean, representing the unconscious. The archetypal patterning of the unconscious I liken to the bottom of the sea, with its variations of depth, terrain, texture, together with vegetation and animal life. The ego-ship on the surface has a scanning mechanism connecting it with the topography and population of the sea floor, influencing the movement of the ego-ship relative to the foundational determinants far below. The archetypal floor does not altogether circumscribe the course of the ego-ship. This is due to the presence on the bridge of the ego-ship captain—will power—which makes decisions within the range of possibilities provided by the archetypal foundation. The ship moves, and the movement modifies its relationship to the archetypal patterns on the sea floor. The sea floor, however, is always there; in no way is it eliminated by the captain. The captain can only make decisions that are related to the archetypal substructure of the sea.

The metaphor cannot be pushed beyond a certain point. A ship is not as dependent upon the floor of the sea as the ego is dependent upon the unconscious. It does suggest, however, that a purpose of psychoanalysis is to aid in the prudent navigation by the ego and its will power within the context of a person's archetypal foundation. To ignore the archetypal foundation and its constitution can be disastrous. It might be called "the Titanic complex." Vaunted ego can come to naught.

When god-phallos enters the range of the ego-ship, it becomes a powerful factor affecting the direction of the ship. This is not the fault of the ego-ship, nor of the shipbuilders (in the story above, the parents) nor the captain (will power). It is the "fault" of the archetype. This is what the parents of the gay children suggest—whether they realize it or not—in their talk of innateness. In spite of their vested interest they make an important point, which the APA, with its bald designation of homosexuality as a "psychological disorder," might do well to consider.

Archetypes do have "faults," especially from the viewpoint of the ego-ship and Captain Will Power of the Titanic. Storms emerging in an instant, icebergs shrouded in fog, rocks that appear without warning, volcanic eruptions, unforeseen windshear—these are archetypal faults, occurring day in and day out in the ordinary lives of human beings. As long as one stays safely in port, the damage may be minimal. There are men who never stray from such refuge. They are those whose containment in the uroboric Great Mother provides them with an illusion of security, like T. S. Eliot's J. Alfred Prufrock, who wondered if he dare eat a peach.[105] The price J. Alfred Prufrock pays for his caution is timidity—the paralysis of erectile prowess.

Entering the realm of god-phallos can be a dangerous business, since the fault of the god may overtake one and lead to possession—an obsessive and/or compulsive infatuation. Ego as solar masculinity has taken precautions regarding chthonic phallos because phallos can be possessed by itself, demanding total ego obeisance, where nothing matters save phallos' orgasmic satisfaction. Apparently this worried Neumann, and caused him to construct an evolution of "lower" phallos into "higher" phallos. He wanted maximum distance between masculine ego consciousness and the voracious appetite of the Great Mother, in whose hands he placed psychic responsibility for chthonic phallos. *It ain't necessarily so.* Phallos has its own split personality, creating on the one hand, rampaging with abandon on the other. Phallos comes close to both its best and worst when it is a battering-ram, hell-bent for orgasmic ecstacy, breaking the barriers of ego safety and defense.

To place the burden of pathology on phallos as such makes no better sense than to place it upon the breast. Is one man more in tow of the Great Mother because he avoids her earthly counterpart while another is less so because he cannot live without her? Is one man frozen in the Great Mother's embrace because he is not drawn to her breast while another is free of her chains because he is?

I have wondered if the sexual preference issue could be resolved by such a simple formula as this: If a man is in need of more father, he is homosexual; if a man is in need of more mother, he is heterosexual; if a man is in need of more of both, he is bisexual. The effort to dictate who a man should love is perverted theology. It is the psychological counterpart of monotheism, dominated by patriarchal triumphalism, demanding adherence to the patriarch's one true god.

It occurred to me once as I trudged my weary bones to still another analytic hour in Zurich, determined to sort out this question, that I never came into a session preoccupied with the pathological desire I had to eat corn flakes for breakfast, rather than healthy granola. Self-preservation and the preservation of the species, eating and sex, are the two basic biological/archetypal instincts. The one takes up almost no time in therapy unless a disorder is involved. The other takes up an enormous amount of time, whether or not a disorder is involved. Something is amiss.

Animus: Phallic Energy in Women

This work has dealt with the foundation of masculine psychology. A few words, however, must be said about how phallos might appear in feminine psychology. No archetype, regardless of gender identification, is solely the experience of one sex or the other. While our bodies tell us that we are male or female without much complication, in the psyche matters are not so simple. Complexity at least makes for a more interesting situation. Moreover, because of the high patriarchal value placed upon masculinity, women may find their complexity is a boon, even as men may find theirs disturbing.

My observations, of course, come from within the context of the masculine standpoint, and are not authenticated in the kind of direct experience that would come from a woman. They are nonetheless offered as an addendum to this work, in an effort to complete a picture. In no sense are they meant to be definitive or even, essentially, correct. In psychology, experience is always the arbiter of truth.

Jung identified the masculine element in a woman's psyche as her animus, which in Latin means mind or spirit. It is equivalent to his concept of anima as the feminine aspect in the male psyche. The Latin *anima* in English means soul, which Jung described as the hidden, inferior, feeling side of a man. Although theoretically it takes a decidedly second place to the masculine (let us say phallic) ego, its presence is felt in a man's moods and emotional reactions. Jung understood anima from the inside, as it were. He could not have understood animus in the same way. He assumed that a woman's animus corresponded functionally to a man's anima, in each case compensating dominant qualities associated with a person's gender identity.[106]

However, Jung was not one to take such an equivalence for granted simply because it neatly evened out the picture. He did observe so-called masculine qualities in the women he knew, and he found them generally inferior to the same qualities he respected in men. He felt just as uneasy about the feminine qualities he found in himself and other men.

Jung attributed the "inferiority" of the contrasexual qualities in both men and women to their repression and neglect. Aspects of one's potential personality that do not fit gender role-modeling drop into the unconscious. They emerge from time to time as typical but undeveloped opposite-sex characteristics. Men, when the ego-guard collapses, tend to be sentimental, fussy, gossipy, querulous—all signs of an anima fit. Similarly, women can be bossy, opinionated, domineering, shallow in thinking—all signs of "animus possession." In women, the supposed guardians of relatedness in a household, such qualities are extremely disruptive. They work against the natural nourishing eros of women, just as self-pity, hysterical overreaction and dramatization work against solar or logos consciousness in men.

So long as this was the extent of animus awareness in Jungian circles, Jung was understood by generations of his followers as demeaning masculine qualities in women. Inferior contrasexual traits in both sexes are indeed a painful reality. But a new generation of Jungian analysts, mostly women—with the late Irene Claremont de Castillejo and Esther Harding as their spiritual mentors—have established women as possessors of an inheritance that takes no back seat to the patriarchy.[107]

Claremont de Castillejo, especially, has been important to me. Her voice was the first I heard raised in protest against Jung's implied

The devil as aerial spirit and ungodly intellect, personification of the negative animus.—Illustration by Eugene Delacroix, 1799-1963. (The Heritage Club, New York)

designation of the animus as soul in women. In *Knowing Woman,* she states that woman's soul too is feminine.[108] To her, soul is always feminine. I understand this to mean that soul gives femininity its authority, since substance and container are one. A woman must look deeply into herself for her soul image.

Animus does not express the essential quality of the female psyche any more than anima expresses the essential quality of the male psyche. Animus in a woman is no longer understood as necessarily negative, but as a multifaceted aspect of the masculine spirit. The so-called negative animus is only a step along the way. Although that step is crucial, animus is more than the cranky inferior masculinity described above . Animus provides a power base for women when it is schooled and disciplined, prepared to be as responsibly solar as is patriarchy at its best. Animus *can* think; it is not shallow when it takes the time and energy necessary for developed thinking.

Women often do deliver collective value judgments and hold undifferentiated opinions—but so do men. In fact, just as men begin to develop emotionally when they stop relying on women to carry eros, so women begin to think individually when they stop depending on men for logos.

What place, then, does phallus-animus have in the creative life of a woman without recourse to a man or masculine image on whom she can project her phallic qualities?

Phallos can be a guide to a woman as he is to a man. His stirring, metaphorically, lets a woman know that creative action is on the horizon. Erection, or the impulse prior to erection (as in the "need to masturbate" in the dream mentioned above) is a sign to a man that something is afoot, that the god is emerging from his slumber. A woman will not feel the pressure from phallos in the same way as a man, yet there are similarities. The stirring of phallos in a man shows his impending readiness to sow seed; in a woman, the positive aspect of animus manifests in impulses to establish herself creatively in the world.

For example, it is animus in a woman that suggests to her, after years of supporting patriarchal structures in routine clerical work, that she herself might have a professional life. It is animus that moves a woman beyond domestic activities and stereotyped "feminine" volunteer work into serious consideration of graduate school and career preparation. Animus moves her to implement such plans and provides the energy to accomplish them. Phallos-animus might jump up, as in an early morning Mercurial erection, desirous of immediate gratification. He can also move slowly and deliberately. A woman is necessarily unfamiliar with phallos as a personal attribute and must be cautious. She may have prior feminine commitments, such as motherhood. When animus shows itself, however, it is unmistakably phallic. In a woman whose femininity is well grounded, animus does not make her masculine. The power element in phallos remains secondary to her feminine receptive nature. Yet it is present and shows itself in her accomplishments.

The development of a woman's inner phallos-animus makes her increasingly independent as a person, particularly in her relationships with men. If a woman is intimately connected to her own masculine resources, she will need to depend less upon the phallic support of an external male.

As I awoke on a summer morning to write this section, wondering what I might say to illustrate the quality of independence in a woman's animus, our Scranton educational radio station was airing interviews with women on the issue of child support after separation. Part of the problem in obtaining adequate child support, aside from the recalcitrant husband, is the difficulty of enforcing court judgments. The women interviewed had independence forced upon them. Neither the fathers of their children nor the patriarchal social structures could be depended upon to provide. These women not only managed well, some of them with numbers of children, but they organized national associations to press for reform of the process. The women sounded strong, determined and proud of themselves. I was reminded of the grim-jawed, hunched-down older woman I recently saw driving a worn Chevrolet along the highway between New York and Scranton. She had one of those octagonal yellow facsimiles of road warning signs dangling in her rear window. It was not the usual "Child on Board" notice. The message was "Ex-husband in Trunk." That woman made my day.

Independence in a woman involves overcoming the constraints imposed by the negative animus. The negative animus is essentially an intrapsychic masculine voice or presence. Though it may appear in the outer world as bothersome temper tantrums inflicted on others, its truly evil colors are known only to the woman herself. Negative animus whispers in a woman's inner ear that she is an incapable idiot, unable to move from her protected state into anything as exalted as "a man's world." If the woman knows what is good for her, she had better play it safe and stick to what she's good at. She is reaching too far and will surely fail; she is meant to support her man and not look out for herself; she is weak and timid, blah, blah, blah. Negative animus functions as phallos-rapist, whose goal is to keep woman in subjection, to subdue her and retaliate for the erotic power she has over him. It is patriarchy in the act of dominating matriarchy.[109]

The development of a negative animus often can be traced to a damaging experience of the personal father (or father-surrogate, as, for example, the mother's animus), but it is by no means fully grasped only in the dynamics of introjection. Behind the personal father stands the world of the archetypal masculine.

Archetypal phallos has a careless, brutal aspect, demanding satisfaction. A woman analysand brought a dream of bugs animatedly copulating on the flowing gown of a classical Greek female statue.

It was a view of phylogenetic development at a primitive stage, superimposed upon a highly sophisticated artifact. The dreamer said to herself in the dream, "In order to penetrate the female, the male needs to rip through the skin with his phallos."

This in-dream interpretation might be viewed from several perspectives. In the case of this woman, and in the context of her therapy, it appeared to me that an aspect of the negative animus was presenting itself in a particularly brutal way—as "ripping through" her skin, and as having a fundamental biological right to do so. Women are continually injured by such an assumption, taking it as a given truth that the masculine voice within them has an authority they dare not question. Feminine archetypal closeness to biology prompts them to submit to indignities visited upon them by the negative animus, whether the imposition appears experientially as physical or psychological.

No woman has but one animus quality in her unconscious household. Indeed, Jung thought that the animus appeared more like a committee of males, implying that a negative animus might live in proximity to positive masculine figures. Thus a woman who dreams of a positive male figure is well advised to build upon his potential for aiding her, in order to counter inner masculine voices that would tear her to pieces. Such figures do come. One woman, beset by depressive bouts during which she worried anxiously about her ability to be an effective manager, had the following dream in which a positive animus figure appeared. As is typical in dreams, she knew the man but consciously would not have considered him a candidate for helping her.

> I am at a big-deal party/dance. A man asks me to dance and I do. We are good at it and he is *very strong*. He lifts me onto my shoulders as we dance, and very nicely. I am very glad he is big enough and strong enough to lead me and lift me that way. [Her emphasis].

Phallos-animus behaves here as he would in a male: he enters the picture autonomously, bidden or unbidden—in this case unbidden. The man in the dream, taken as a subjective image of the dreamer's animus, both affirms her femininity and provides her with an indication of her own phallic strength. The woman's job is to trust this "very strong" animus, as a man must trust the urging and presence of phallos.

There are intrinsic limitations to what a man may say with authority about a woman's animus, whether negative or, in my terms, phallic-positive. My views here, although informed by what women have written on the subject and by my own experience, are conditioned by my masculine identity, however much my personal anima may have experienced similar patriarchal efforts to intrude or support. I look forward to further elucidation, by women themselves, of how the feminine experiences phallic energy.

Epilogue

In the foregoing pages I have emphasized the religious importance of phallos. Theoretically, Jungians have a way of understanding this. It remains to be seen whether others will find the connection with religion compelling or even comprehensible.

It may be helpful to remember that religion, in the Jungian view of the psyche, is a nontheological construct, a creative manifestation of the "not-I," as Esther Harding called the unconscious.[110] Phallos as co-original with the maternal principle, numinous, object of fascination and devotion, and signature of gender identity for half the human race, requires its placement within a construct capable of containing and elucidating those attributes.

The implications of phallos for psychotherapy are scattered throughout this book. At this point I need only say that the acceptance of phallos as a foundational psychic image makes analysis a more honest procedure, less apt to veer unconsciously in a patriarchal direction, more likely to facilitate the conscious integration—in both men and women—of archetypal masculine qualities.

There are broader implications. At a time of waning patriarchal values, cultural presuppositions are in a great flux. It may be that humanity is moving inexorably toward *unus mundus,* a new union of opposites, postmatriarchal and postpatriarchal, that gives equal weight to the masculine and the feminine. If so, elements of psychological fundament long neglected must be consciously included for the evolution to be complete. My conviction is that an understanding of *phallos protos* or patrix, coequal with the feminine matrix, will be crucial to this new age.

Notes

CW—*The Collected Works of C.G. Jung*

1. Theodor Reik, *Listening with the Third Ear,* p. xi.
2. George Elder, "Phallus," p. 1.
3. Jung, *Symbols of Transformation,* CW 5, par. 669 and note.
4. See Arnold Mindell, *Dreambody.*
5. Jung, *Two Essays on Analytical Psychology,* p. 123.
6. Mircea Eliade, *Images and Symbols,* p. 9.
7. Ibid., p. 14.
8. See above, note 1.
9. Jung, *Psychological Types,* CW 6, par. 789.
10. Rudolf Otto, *The Idea of the Holy,* p. xvi (translator's preface).
11. Ibid., p. 7.
12. Ibid., p. xvi.
13. Ibid., chapters 4-6.
14. Thomas Wright, "A Worship of the Generative Powers," p. 28.
15. Jung, *Symbols of Transformation,* CW 5, par. 146.
16. Alain Daniélou, *Shiva and Dionysus,* p. 56.
17. Ibid.
18. Ibid.
19. Ibid.
20. Ibid., p. 58.
21. See above, note 15.
22. Thorkil Vanggaard, *Phallos,* p. 16.
23. John Sharkey, *Celtic Mysteries: The Ancient Religion,* text for plate 9.
24. Galatians 5:16-17; Authorized (King James) Version.
25. See Jung, "Answer to Job," *Psychology and Religion,* CW 11.
26. Sigmund Freud, "Analysis Terminable and Interminable," pp. 250-252.
27. See Marie-Louise von Franz, *Puer Aeternus: The Adult Struggle with the Paradise of Childhood,* and Daryl Sharp, *The Secret Raven: Conflict and Transformation.*
28. Jung, *Memories, Dreams, Reflections,* pp. 26-27.
29. Ibid., pp. 27-28.

30. Jung's views on this subject appear most extensively in *Symbols of Transformation,* CW 5; see especially part 2, chapters 4-8.

31. In *C.G. Jung: His Myth in Our Time* (pp. 15-37), Marie-Louise von Franz comments extensively on Jung's early phallic dream. She sees it as an indication of his strong eros factor, his love of people, his marked religious outlook coming upon him as a child, and, most importantly, as an antecedent of his appreciation for the "light of nature," the instinctual unconscious. She also understands this dream as an early indication of Jung's conviction that God is not dead but rather buried in the unconscious, awaiting human discovery. She does not deal at any length with its sexual significance but rather emphasizes its portent for creativity and masculine spiritual insemination.

32. See Erich Neumann, *The Origins and History of Consciousness,* p. 42.

33. Quoted in ibid., pp. 47-48.

34. Freud, *The Future of an Illusion,* p. 26.

35. George Hogenson, *Jung's Struggle with Freud,* pp. 84-85.

36. James Hillman, *Re-Visioning Psychology,* pp. 84ff.

37. John Money and Anke Ehrhardt, *Man and Woman, Boy and Girl,* pp. 7, 147-148.

38. Jung, *Memories, Dreams, Reflections,* p. 182.

39. It has been suggested that Jung had some difficulty controlling his sexual activity in his middle years. See, for example, Aldo Carotenuto, *A Secret Symmetry: Sabina Spielrein Between Jung and Freud.*

40. Erich Neumann's three major works are *The Origins and History of Consciousness, The Great Mother* and *Depth Psychology and a New Ethic.* Although in print in the United States for over twenty-five years, they have yet to be discovered by the general American psychoanalytic community. Neumann was born in Berlin in 1905; he left Germany in 1933 and died in Israel in 1960 (a year before Jung's death). His early death was a great loss to analytical psychology.

41. Neumann, *The Origins and History of Consciousness,* p. 92.

42. Ibid., p. 309.

43. Ibid.

44. Ibid., p. 10.

45. Neumann, *The Great Mother,* p. 294.

46. T.S. Eliot, "Little Gidding," *Four Quartets.*

47. Aniela Jaffé, *Jung's Last Years and Other Essays,* p. 7.

48. Jung, "A Psychological View of Conscience," *Civilization in Transition,* CW 10, par. 852.

49. Jung, *Mysterium Coniunctionis,* CW 14, par. 788: "It seems to me . . . reasonable to take cognizance of the fact that there is not only a psychic but a psychoid unconscious."

50. Mitchell Wilson and the editors of *Life* magazine, *Energy,* p. 143.

51. Ibid., p. 144.

52. Jung, "Synchronicity: An Acausal Connecting Principle," *The Structure and Dynamics of the Psyche,* CW 8, par. 964.

53. Marion Woodman, *The Pregnant Virgin,* p. 39.

54. Jung, *Mysterium Coniunctionis,* CW 14, par. 786.

55. See Jung, "The Transcendent Function," *The Structure and Dynamics of the Psyche,* CW 8.

56. Jung, "The Spirit Mercurius," *Alchemical Studies,* CW 13, par. 263.

57. Roger Cook, *The Tree of Life,* p. 9.

58. Mircea Eliade, *Shamanism,* p. 210.

59. Ibid., p. 169.

60. Ibid., p. 259.

61. Rafael Lopez-Pedraza, *Hermes and His Children,* p. 3.

62. Hodder M. Westropp and C. Stanaland Wake, *Phallicism in Ancient Worship,* p. 50.

63. George Elder, "Phallus," p. 5.

64. Jung, "The Spirit Mercurius," *Alchemical Studies,* CW 13, par. 239.

65. Ibid., par. 278.

66. Ibid., par. 284.

67. Ibid., par. 287.

68. See Marion Woodman, *Addiction to Perfection,* chapter 8, "The Ravished Bride."

69. *Vocatus atque non vocatus, Deus aderit* (Called or not, God will be present).

70. Jung also presents, in *Psychology and Alchemy* (CW 12, fig. 231), a sixteenth-century drawing of Mercurius as virgin, standing erect, with the branches of the *arbor philosophica* emerging from his/her head. Here is bisexual Mercurius, consisting, in Jung's words, "of all conceivable opposites." Mercurius as virgin suggests an identification of tree as mother-bearer, an implication it is difficult altogether to escape. Regarding Mercurius himself, the propensity he has to transform himself into a female only adds to his availability as an

image of the Self (as Jung suggests). This matter will be taken up in my discussion of Dionysus.

71. Stanislas K. de Rola, *Alchemy: The Secret Art,* plate 39; see also Jung, *Psychology and Alchemy,* CW 12, fig. 131.

72. Jung, *Psychology and Alchemy,* CW 12, caption to fig. 131.

73. Walter F. Otto, *Dionysus: Myth and Cult,* p. 180.

74. Ibid., p. 176.

75. Ibid., p. 178.

76. *The New Larousse Encyclopedia of Mythology,* p. 161.

77. Karl Kerényi, commentary in Paul Radin, *The Trickster: A Study in American Indian Mythology,* p. 190.

78. *The New Larousse,* p. 137.

79. Ibid., p. 138.

80. Ibid., p. 98.

81. Jung, *Aion,* CW 9ii, par. 219.

82. Ibid., par. 220.

83. D.H. Lawrence, *Women in Love,* p. 231.

84. Ibid., p. 541.

85. Jung, *Two Essays on Analytical Psychology,* CW 7, par. 103, note.

86. Ibid., par. 152.

87. Amanda Spake, "The End of the Ride," p. 40.

88. Quoted by Keith Thompson in "What Men Really Want: A *New Age* Interview with Robert Bly," p. 32.

89. Ibid., p. 33.

90. *The Complete Grimm's Fairy Tales,* pp. 612-620.

91. John Donne, *Selected Poems.*

92. For discussion of this theme from a woman's point of view, see Marion Woodman, *Addiction to Perfection,* chapter 8, "The Ravished Bride."

93. See Fox Butterfield, "College Sexual Assault Case Stirs Massachusetts," *New York Times,* July 2, 1986.

94. Jung, *Two Essays on Analytical Psychology,* CW 7, pars. 254ff.

95. Jung, "Transformation Symbolism in the Mass," *Psychology and Religion,* CW 11.

96. I am aware that the Kundalini—the inner life force in Indian tantra—is understood as feminine energy. I take some liberties with this traditional understanding, since the energy of phallos in this dream, and generally, appears to be similar to the movement of the Kundalini. It may be that as seen from the psychoid perspective, the two are,

indeed, one. Furthermore, it is interesting to speculate that the *lingam-phallos*, around which the Kundalini is traditionally coiled—covering "his" mouth with "hers"—is the power source of Kundalini energy.

97. See, for instance, Ajit Mookerjee and Madhu Khanna, *The Tantric Way*.

98. *The Shorter Catechism,* Question 1 (7.001).

99. John Boswell, "Homosexuality, Religious Life and the Clergy."

100. See above, note 22.

101. See "Crime in the Bedroom," editorial, *New York Times,* July 2, 1986.

102. For example, Ephesians 5:22-32.

103. Boswell, *Christianity, Social Tolerance and Homosexuality, p. 251.*

104. *New York Times,* article by Sandra Blakeslee, August 26, 1985.

105. T.S. Eliot, "The Love Song of J. Alfred Prufrock": "Shall I part my hair behind? Do I dare to eat a peach? / I shall wear white flannel trousers, and walk upon the beach."

106. Jung, "The Syzygy: Anima and Animus," *Aion,* CW 9ii, pars. 20-42.

107. See Irene Claremont de Castillejo, *Knowing Woman,* and M. Esther Harding, *The Way of All Women* and *Woman's Mysteries, Ancient and Modern.*

108. Claremont de Castillejo, *Knowing Woman,* pp. 165ff.

109. See Marion Woodman, *The Pregnant Virgin,* chapter two, "'Taking It Like a Man': Abandonment in the Creative Woman."

110. M. Esther Harding, *The I and the Not-I.*

Bibliography

Bachofen, J.J. *Das Mutterrecht: Eine Untersuchung über die Gynaikokratie der alten Welt nach ihrer religiosen und rechtlichen Natur* (1861). English translation: *Myth, Religion and the Mother Right* (Bollingen Series LXXXIV). Trans. Ralph Manheim. Princeton University Press, Princeton, 1967.

Boswell, John. *Christianity, Social Tolerance and Homosexuality: Gay People in Western Europe from the Beginning of the Christian Era to the Fourteenth Century.* University of Chicago Press, Chicago, 1980.

––––––. "Homosexuality, Religious Life and the Clergy." Tape recording of presentation at Symposium II, November 8-10, 1985. New Ways Ministry, Mt. Rainier, Maryland, 1985.

Carotenuto, Aldo. *A Secret Symmetry: Sabina Spielrein Between Jung and Freud.* Trans. Arno Pomerans, John Shepley, Krishna Winston. Pantheon Books, New York, 1982.

Claremont de Castillejo, Irene. *Knowing Woman: A Feminine Psychology.* G.P. Putnam's Sons for C.G. Jung Foundation for Analytical Psychology, New York, 1973.

Cook, Roger. *The Tree of Life.* Avon Books, New York, 1974.

Daniélou, Alain. *Shiva and Dionysus: The Religion of Nature and Eros.* Trans. K.F. Hurry. Inner Traditions International, New York, 1984.

De Rola, Stanislas Klossowski. *Alchemy: The Secret Art.* Avon Books, New York, 1973.

Donne, John. *Selected Poems.* Ed. Matthias A. Shaaber. Appleton-Century-Crofts, New York, 1958.

Elder, George R. "Phallus." Article submitted for publication in *The Encyclopedia of Religion.* Ed. Mircea Eliade. The Free Press, New York (forthcoming).

Eliade, Mircea. *Images and Symbols.* Trans. Philip Mairet. Sheed and Ward, New York, 1969.

––––––. *Shamanism: Archaic Techniques of Ecstasy* (Bollingen Series LXXVI). Trans. Willard R. Trask. Pantheon Books, New York, 1964.

Eliot, T.S. *The Complete Poems and Plays.* Harcourt, Brace and Co., New York, 1952.

Freud, Sigmund. "Analysis Terminable and Interminable." In *The Standard Edition of the Complete Psychological Works of Sigmund Freud,* vol. 23. Ed. James Strachey, Anna Freud. Hogarth Press, London, 1961.

––––––. *The Future of an Illusion.* Trans. W.D. Robson-Scott. Ed. Ernest Jones. Liveright Publishing Corp., New York, 1949.

Grimm's Fairy Tales, The Complete. Routledge and Kegan Paul, London, 1975.

Harding, M. Esther. *The I and the Not-I* (Bollingen Series LXXIX). Princeton University Press, Princeton, 1965.

————. *The Way of All Women*. Harper Colophon, New York, 1975.

————. *Woman's Mysteries, Ancient and Modern*. Harper and Row, New York, 1976.

Hillman, James. *Re-Visioning Psychology*. Harper and Row, New York, 1975.

Hogenson, George B. *Jung's Struggle with Freud*. Notre Dame Press, Notre Dame, 1983.

Jaffé, Aniela. *Jung's Last Years and Other Essays*. Trans. R.F.C. Hull, Murray Stein. Spring Publications, Dallas, 1984.

Jung, C.G. *The Collected Works* (Bollingen Series XX). 20 vols. Trans. R.F.C. Hull. Ed. H. Read, M. Fordham, G. Adler, Wm. McGuire. Princeton University Press, Princeton, 1953-1979.

————. *Memories, Dreams, Reflections*. Trans. Richard and Clara Winston. Ed. Aniela Jaffé. Pantheon Books, New York, 1963.

Larousse Encyclopedia of Mythology, New. Hamlyn, London, 1968.

Lawrence, D.H. *Women in Love*. Penguin Books, Harmondsworth, 1976.

Lopez-Pedraza, Rafael. *Hermes and His Children*. Spring Publications, Zurich, 1977.

Mindell, Arnold. *Dreambody: The Body's Role in Revealing the Self*. Sigo Press, Boston, 1981.

Money, John and Ehrhardt, Anke A. *Man and Woman, Boy and Girl*. Johns Hopkins University Press, Baltimore, 1972.

Mookerjee, Ajit and Khanna, Madhu. *The Tantric Way: Art, Science, Ritual*. Thames and Hudson, London, 1977.

Neumann, Erich. *Depth Psychology and a New Ethic*. G.P. Putnam's Sons, New York, 1969.

————. *The Great Mother: An Analysis of the Archetype* (Bollingen Series XLVII). Trans. Ralph Manheim. Princeton University Press, Princeton, 1972.

————. *The Origins and History of Consciousness* (Bollingen Series XLII). Trans. R.F.C. Hull. Princeton University Press, Princeton, 1970.

Otto, Rudolf. *The Idea of the Holy*. Trans. John W. Harvey. Oxford University Press, London, 1923.

Otto, Walter F. *Dionysus: Myth and Cult*. Trans. Robert B. Palmer. Indiana University Press, Bloomington, 1965.

Radin, Paul. *The Trickster: A Study in American Indian Mythology.* Commentaries by Karl Kerényi and C.G. Jung. Schocken Books, New York, 1972.

Reik, Theodor. *Listening with the Third Ear: The Inner Experience of a Psychoanalyst.* Farrar, Straus and Co., New York, 1949.

Sharkey, John. *Celtic Mysteries: The Ancient Religion.* Avon Books, New York, 1975.

Sharp, Daryl. *The Secret Raven: Conflict and Transformation.* Inner City Books, Toronto, 1980.

Shorter Catechism, The. 2nd ed. Part One, Book of Confessions. Office of the General Assembly, United Presbyterian Church, Philadelphia, 1970.

Spake, Amanda. "The End of the Ride: Analyzing a Sex Crime." In *Sex, Porn and Male Rage,* special issue of *Mother Jones,* April 1980.

Thompson, Keith. "What Men Really Want: A *New Age* Interview with Robert Bly." In *New Age,* May 1982.

Vanggaard, Thorkil. *Phallos: A Symbol and Its History in the Male World.* International University Press, Independence, Missouri, 1972.

Von Franz, Marie-Louise. *C.G. Jung: His Myth in Our Time.* Trans. William H. Kennedy. Hodder and Stoughton, New York, 1975.

———. *Puer Aeternus: The Adult Struggle with the Paradise of Childhood.* 2nd ed. Sigo Press, Santa Monica, 1981.

Westropp, Hodder M. and Wake, C. Stanaland. *Phallicism in Ancient Worship.* J.W. Bouton, New York, 1875.

Wilson, Mitchell and the editors of *Life* magazine. *Energy.* Life Science Library (Time, Inc.), New York, 1963.

Woodman, Marion. *Addiction to Perfection: The Still Unravished Bride.* Inner City Books, Toronto, 1982.

———. *The Pregnant Virgin: A Process of Psychological Transformation.* Inner City Books, Toronto, 1985.

Wright, Thomas. "A Worship of the Generative Powers" (1866). Reprinted in Richard Payne Knight and Thomas Wright, *Sexual Symbolism: A History of Phallic Worship.* The Julian Press, New York, 1957.

Index

Numbers in italics refer to illustrations

136

Studies in Jungian Psychology
by Jungian Analysts

Quality Paperbacks

Prices and payment in $US (except in Canada, $Cdn)

1. The Secret Raven: Conflict and Transformation
Daryl Sharp (Toronto). ISBN 0-919123-00-7. 128 pp. $16

2. The Psychological Meaning of Redemption Motifs in Fairy Tales
Marie-Louise von Franz (Zürich). ISBN 0-919123-01-5. 128 pp. $16

3. On Divination and Synchronicity: The Psychology of Meaningful Chance
Marie-Louise von Franz (Zürich). ISBN 0-919123-02-3. 128 pp. $16

4. The Owl Was a Baker's Daughter: Obesity, Anorexia and the Repressed Feminine Marion Woodman (Toronto). ISBN 0-919123-03-1. 144 pp. $16

5. Alchemy: An Introduction to the Symbolism and the Psychology
Marie-Louise von Franz (Zürich). ISBN 0-919123-04-X. 288 pp. $20

6. Descent to the Goddess: A Way of Initiation for Women
Sylvia Brinton Perera (New York). ISBN 0-919123-05-8. 112 pp. $16

7. The Psyche as Sacrament: A Comparative Study of C.G. Jung and Paul Tillich John P. Dourley (Ottawa). ISBN 0-919123-06-6. 128 pp. $16

8. Border Crossings: Carlos Castaneda's Path of Knowledge
Donald Lee Williams (Boulder). ISBN 0-919123-07-4. 160 pp. $16

9. Narcissism and Character Transformation: The Psychology of Narcissistic Character Disorders
Nathan Schwartz-Salant (New York). ISBN 0-919123-08-2. 192 pp. $18

10. Rape and Ritual: A Psychological Study
Bradley A. Te Paske (Santa Barbara). ISBN 0-919123-09-0. 160 pp. $16

11. Alcoholism and Women: The Background and the Psychology
Jan Bauer (Montreal). ISBN 0-919123-10-4. 144 pp. $16

12. Addiction to Perfection: The Still Unravished Bride
Marion Woodman (Toronto). ISBN 0-919123-11-2. 208 pp. $18pb/$25hc

13. Jungian Dream Interpretation: A Handbook of Theory and Practice
James A. Hall, M.D. (Dallas). ISBN 0-919123-12-0. 128 pp. $16

14. The Creation of Consciousness: Jung's Myth for Modern Man
Edward F. Edinger (Los Angeles). ISBN 0-919123-13-9. 128 pp. $16

15. The Analytic Encounter: Transference and Human Relationship
Mario Jacoby (Zürich). ISBN 0-919123-14-7. 128 pp. $16

16. Change of Life: Dreams and the Menopause
Ann Mankowitz (Ireland). ISBN 0-919123-15-5. 128 pp. $16

17. The Illness That We Are: A Jungian Critique of Christianity
John P. Dourley (Ottawa). ISBN 0-919123-16-3. 128 pp. $16

18. Hags and Heroes: A Feminist Approach to Jungian Psychotherapy with Couples Polly Young-Eisendrath (Philadelphia). ISBN 0-919123-17-1. 192 pp. $18

19. Cultural Attitudes in Psychological Perspective
Joseph L. Henderson, M.D. (San Francisco). ISBN 0-919123-18-X. 128 pp. $16

20. The Vertical Labyrinth: Individuation in Jungian Psychology
Aldo Carotenuto (Rome). ISBN 0-919123-19-8. 144 pp. $16

Discounts: any 3-5 books, 10%; 6-9 books, 20%; 10 or more, 25%

Add Postage/Handling: 1-2 books, $3; 3-4 books, $5; 5-9 books, $10; 10 or more, free

Credit cards: Contact BookWorld toll-free: 1-800-444-2524, or Fax 1-800-777-2525

Free **Catalogue** with over **100** titles, and **Jung at Heart** newsletter

INNER CITY BOOKS, Box 1271, Station Q, Toronto, ON M4T 2P4, Canada
Tel. 416-927-0355 / Fax: 416-924-1814 / E-mail: icb@inforamp.net